An Outline of

CLASSICAL MYTHOLOGY

ROBERT E. WOLVERTON

About the Author

Received his A.B. in Classical Languages and Literature from Hanover College, his A.M. from the University of Michigan and his Ph.D. from the University of North Carolina. He has held teaching positions at the University of Georgia, Tufts University, and Florida State University. As the recipient of one of the first twenty-five Fellowships in the Academic Administration Internship Program, sponsored by the American Council on Education, Dr. Wolverton spent the academic year 1965-66 as an Assistant to the President of Mills College.

Publications:

Dr. Wolverton has published articles, reviews and translations for *Classical Journal, Classical Outlook, American Historical Review,* and *Eleusis.* Recent articles are included in *Classical, Medieval and Renaissance Studies in Honor of B. L. Ullman,* and in *Studies in Honor of W. E. Caldwell.* His book, *Classical Elements in English Words,* appeared in 1965 as a Littlefield, Adams & Co. Quality Paperback.

About the Book

The aim of this volume is to present Greek and Roman myths in a logical, sequential order, rather than in a manner of a dictionary or reference work. As an outline, it does not contain the many variants of the myths, nor does it endeavor to compare classical myths with those of other countries. The introductory chapter will give the reader a thumb-nail review of Greek and Latin literature, and the select bibliography will refer him to other readily available works. Between the Introduction and the Bibliography will be found an interesting and coherent account of the stories which adorned contemporary art, drama and literature, and which have enhanced subsequent art, drama, literature and music.

Dedicated to Those

of All Ages

Who Love Ageless Stories

An Outline of

CLASSICAL MYTHOLOGY

ROBERT E. WOLVERTON

Florida State University

1966

LITTLEFIELD, ADAMS & CO.

Totowa, New Jersey

Printed in the United States of America

Preface

As the title suggests, this is an outline of classical mythology, not a comprehensive compendium of facts, nor a startlingly original analysis. If I were called upon to justify such an outline, I would do so on the grounds that organization is important in any field, but especially in the field of mythology, where one can be so easily led in all directions at the same time. This volume, then, is an attempt to organize classical mythology into a logical pattern of subjects. It came about as the result of my teaching a course in this field for a number of years; in so doing, I found some middle course between the Scylla of simply retelling of stories and the Charybdis of a too scholarly analysis which would perhaps deprive the myths of their lively charm. Hopefully, that course, or that Sophoclean balance, is reflected by the present volume.

In answer to the question so frequently put to me, "What is *your* definition of myth?," I would say that a myth is the ancestral prototype of some experience. My own study has convinced me that any restrictive or descriptive definition of myth is inadequate. But however they may be defined and whatever their origin, all myths breathe a vitality which mainly grew from the Greek genius for story-telling. The bards who sang or told the stories were real geniuses at "creative borrowing," able to take the skeleton of an idea, a character, an incident, an emotion, or a situation and to clothe it with their individual and imaginative patterns. Homer has always been cited as the supreme example of such a bard; yet, to paraphrase Horace, there must have been great poets before Homer, men who transmitted the stories from one generation to another. Thus, transmission, repetition, and freedom to "ad lib" gave the myths new meanings affecting many nations all over the world at all times. So myths have continued their elusive and intriguing way, evoking speculations, inviting interpretations, and enriching human imaginations.

Finally, a word of explanation is due to the reader who may wonder why the same figure appears with differently spelled or variant names. The reason is that a different context seemed naturally to demand the alternate spelling or form. For the most part, however, Anglicized versions of Greek names have been used because they are more familiar; thus Heracles rather than Herakles, and, where more appropriate, Hercules rather than Heracles.

Before concluding, I must express my thanks to those students of Florida State University who continually reminded me of the sheer joy of studying classical mythology, as they eagerly learned the catalogue of all the strange-sounding names. To my patient wife a word of thanks for always keeping me far removed from *hubris* and for suggestions which were invariably valid. To Mrs. Kay Stops my deepest gratitude is owed, for without her Olympian calm, skill and competence, this work would not have been possible; every office should be blessed with at least one person of such insight, knowledge, and efficiency.

R. E. W.

TABLE OF CONTENTS

Ancient Sources for Classical Mythology

I. GREEK AUTHORS

A. Preclassical Period, c. 850-c. 500 B. C.

1. Homer (c. 850) : Iliad; Odyssey (24 books each)
2. Epic (Trojan) Cycle:
   - (a.) Cypria (11 bks.) ; Events leading up to the Trojan War and during the first nine years of the war.
   - (b.) Aethiopis (5 bks.) : Post-Iliad events, including the arrival of the Amazons and the deaths of Penthesilea, Memnon and Achilles; quarrel for arms of Achilles between Ajax and Odysseus.
   - (c.) Little Iliad (4 bks.) : Awarding of Achilles' arms to Odysseus, madness and suicide of Ajax, and the taking of the Wooden Horse into Troy.
   - (d.) Sack of Ilium (2 bks.) ; Capture of Troy and departure of Greeks with booty.
   - (e.) Nostoi (Returns) (5 bks.) : Fortunes of Neoptolemus, Calchas, Nestor, Diomedes and others; death of Agamemnon.
   - (f.) Telegonia (2 bks.) ; Sequel to the Odyssey; Telegonus, son of Odysseus by Circe, accidentally kills Odysseus; he then marries Penelope and Telemachus marries Circe; Circe makes them all immortal.
3. Other epics, not dealing with the Trojan War.
   - (a.) Titanomachia (at least 2 bks.) : How Zeus became lord of the universe.
   - (b.) Oedipodea (6600 lines) : Story of Oedipus.
   - (c.) Thebais (7000 lines) : Events leading up to the first attack of the Seven Against Thebes; battle at Thebes which ended in the deaths of six of the seven attacking leaders.
   - (d.) Epigoni: Second, and successful, attack against Thebes by the sons of the original Seven.

With the exception of Homer's Iliad and Odyssey, all the above works are known only in fragments or from secondary sources. Yet, they were important works because of their influence upon the later literature of the Greeks and Romans.

4. Homeric Hymns: 33 in all, of various dates and localities. i., To Dionysos; ii., To Demeter; iii., To Apollo (vss. 1-178, to Apollo of Delos; vss. 179-end, to Apollo of Delphi) ; iv., To Hermes; v., To Aphrodite; vi., To Aphrodite; vii., To Dionysos; viii., To Ares; ix., To Artemis; x., To Aphrodite; xi., To Athena; xii., To Hera; xiii., To Demeter; xiv., To the Mother of the Gods; xv., To Herakles Lion-Hearted; xvi., To Asklepios; xvii., To the Dioskuroi; xviii., To Hermes; xix., To Pan; xx., To Hephaistos; xxi., To Apollo; xxii., To Poseidon; xxiii., To Zeus; xxiv., To Hestia; xxv., To the Muses and Apollo; xxvi., To Dionysos; xxvii., To Artemis; xxviii., To Athena; xxix To Hestia; xxx., To Earth, the Mother of all; xxxi., To Helios; xxxii., To Selene; xxxiii., To the Dioskuroi.

5. Hesiod (c. 750) :
   (a.) Works and Days, an open letter on the need for justice and the honor of labor; includes the myths of Pandora and the Five Ages of Mankind.
   (b.) Theogony, the earliest attempted geneology of the gods; many names, representing many lands, times and beliefs: a patch-work catalogue.
   (c.) Catalogue of Women (at least 5 bks.) , now only in fragmentary form.

6. pseudo-Hesiod: Shield of Herakles (480 vss.) ; 178 verses describe the shield made by Hephaistos for Herakles.

7. Elegiac poets: Callinus, Mimnermus, Tyrtaeus of Sparta, Solon, Theognis.

8. Iambic poets: Archilochus, Hipponax.

9. Lyric poets: Sappho (a genius-poetess) , Alcaeus, Anacreon, Terpander (an inventor of music) , Alcman, Arion, Stesichorus, Ibycus, Simonides of Ceos.

B. Classical Period, c. 500-c. 300 B. C.

1. Pindar (c. 520-c. 440) : Olympian, Pythian, Nemean, Isthmian Odes; written in honor of victors at the four great Pan-Hellenic games; his ode form came to be called the Pindaric Ode.

2. Bacchylides (c. 505-c. 450) : Odes, to victors of the Pan-Hellenic games; somewhat easier reading than Pindar; Dithyrambs, the forerunners of drama.

3. Herodotus (c. 480-c. 425), "father of history:" History of the Persian Wars (9 bks., each named for a Muse); though really a history, the work is also a travelogue by an inquisitive tourist.

4. Thucydides (c. 460-c. 400), "father of analytic history:" History of the Peloponnesian War (8 bks.); one of the most important works in Western literature, an accurate analysis of humans and their behavior.

5. Aeschylus (525-456): Tragedies (only 7 extant of his nearly 90): Suppliants, Persians, Seven Against Thebes, Prometheus Bound; the Oresteian trilogy, Agamemnon, Choephoroe, and Eumenides. An innovator in tragedy, he wished to be remembered as a patriot.

6. Sophocles (496-406): Tragedies (7 extant out of some 120): Antigone, Oedipus the King, Electra, Ajax, Trachinian Women, Philoctetes, Oedipus at Colonus; large fragments of a satyr-play, the Trackers, survive. Also an innovator in tragedy, highly regarded in his own day, and on everyone's "favorite author" list.

7. Euripides (c. 480-406): Tragedies (18 extant of some 80 to 90): Rhesus, Alcestis, Medea, Hippolytus, Trojan Women, Helen, Orestes, Iphigenia at Aulis, Bacchae, Andromache, Children of Herakles, Hecuba, Suppliants, Electra, Madness of Herakles, Iphigenia in Tauris, Ion, Phoenissae; a satyr-play, Cyclops. Interested in psychological studies, especially of women, and irrational forces of life.

8. Aristophanes (c. 448-c. 380); Comedies (11 extant of some 44): Acharnians, Knights, Clouds, Wasps, Peace, Birds, Lysistrata, Thesmophoriazusae, Frogs, Ecclesiazusae, Plutus. Wise and witty, the thinking man's comedian.

9. Xenophon (c. 430-c. 355): easy-to-read works on various subjects:
   (a.) Anabasis, the original "you are there" war journal.
   (b.) Memorabilia, Apology, and Symposium, which include his recollections of Socrates.
   (c.) Oeconomicus, concerning his home life.
   (d.) Cyropaedia, training of Cyrus and experiences in Persia.
   (e.) The Cavalry Commander, Horsemanship, On Hunting, all "how-to" works.
   (f.) Hellenica, or history of Greece.

10. Plato (c. 427-347), an intellectual giant, author of Dialogues and Letters, all of which are extant: Apology, Crito, Charmides, Laches, Euthyphro, Hippias Minor, Hippias Major (?), Ion, (all, taken together, called the Socratic Group); Gorgias, Pro-

tagoras, Euthydemus, Cratylus, Phaedo, Republic, Meno, Alcibiades (?), Menexenus, Phaedrus, Symposium, Theaetetus, Parmenides, (all often referred to as the First and Second Platonic Groups) ; Sophist, Politicus, Timaeus, Critias, Philebus, Laws (the Third Platonic Group). The *Republic* still remains in the "must read" category.

11. Aristotle (384-322), another intellectual giant, author of a vast number of works on varied subjects, works generally divided into two classes, esoteric and exoteric. His extant treatises may be categorized as follows: on logic, on metaphysics, on natural philosophy, on ethics and politics, and on rhetoric and poetry.

C. Hellenistic Period, c. 300-c. 100 B. C.

1. Callimachus (born c. 310) : 6 Hymns (to Zeus, Apollo, Artemis, Delos, Pallas, Demeter) ; Aitia (Causes or Origins, now only in fragments) ; Hecale (an epyllion or little epic) ; Lock of Berenice; Epigrams. A literary rival of Apollonius of Rhodes, he was the author of the proverb, "a large book is a large nuisance."
2. Appollonius of Rhodes (c. 295-215) : Argonautica (4 bks.)
3. Euhemerus (fl. c. 300) : The Sacred Record and On Incredible Tales, both of which have been called by literary critics "foolish," "stupid," and "trash." He put forth the theory, later named for him, that the Greek gods had their origins in human princes or other notables who had been deified after their death.
4. Theocritus (fl. c. 270) : Idylls, the first pastoral poems, of which the best known are: i (the death of Daphnis) ; xi (Cyclops, which treats of the story of Polyphemus and Galatea) ; xv (Women at the Adonia) . Two of his 3 or 4 epyllia were Epithalamium of Helen and Infant Herakles.
5. Bion (c. 100?) : 6 Idylls, one being a Lament for Adonis.
6. Moschus (c. 150) : Idylls, including the story of Europa and a Lament for Bion.

D. Roman Period, c. 100 B. C. to c. 500 A. D.

1. Diodorus Siculus (fl. in age of Augustus) : Library of History (40 bks.) , a world history from mythical times to c. 59 B. C. He traces many gods back to Egypt or to mortals who had benefited mankind.
2. Dionysius of Halicarnassus (fl. 30-5 B. C.) : History of Rome (11 bks. extant, fragments from 9 more) ; and, several works on literary criticism.

3. Plutarch (c. 46 A. D.-c. 120 A. D.) : Moralia, a large collection of various essays; and, the Parallel Lives, one of the preeminent books of the world.

4. Apollodorus (pseudo-) (early Roman Empire) : Library, a work which, though faulty, is a prime source for Greek mythology. There was an earlier Apollodorus (of Athens), who was a prolific writer on grammar, mythology, geography, and history.

5. Lucian (c. 115-c. 200 A. D.), whose diversity make his writings fall into these classifications:
    (a.) rhetorical exercises, including 2 speeches entitled Phalaris.
    (b.) works on literary subjects.
    (c.) quasi-philosophic works, including Dialogues of the Dead, Charon, Descent into Hades, Menippus, Cock, Confutation of Zeus, Sale of Lives, and Fisher.
    (d.) satirical dialogues, such as Dialogues of Courtesans, Dialogues of the Gods, and Concerning the Syrian Goddess.
    (e.) miscellaneous works, such as Lucius, the Ass, and Ocypus, a parody on the name of Oedipus.

6. Pausanias (second half of 2nd century A. D.) : Description of Greece (10 bks.), a valuable guide-book for tourists and students.

7. Philostratus (2nd and 3rd centuries A. D.) : Imagines (2 bks.), descriptions of 66 paintings; and, Letters, in one of which appears "Drink to me only with thine eyes."

8. Nonnus (c. 400 A. D.) : Dionysiaca (48 bks.), an epic about Dionysus.

II. LATIN AUTHORS

A. Early Period, c. 250-c. 40 B. C.

1. Livius Andronicus (fl. c. 240) : translation of the Odyssey into Latin verse; introduced drama to Romans; only fragments survive.

2. Ennius (239-169), versatile "father of Latin Poetry:" Annals (18 bks.), a history of Rome; Saturae, miscellaneous pieces; Epicharmus, on the physical make-up of the universe; Euhemerus, in which he accepts the rationalistic theory on the origins of the gods.

3. Plautus (c. 254-184), witty and humorous Comedies (20 or 21 out of 130 survive); his Amphitruo had profound influence on subsequent plays treating the theme of the birth of Hercules.

4. Cicero (106-43), orator, politician, statesman: Letters; Orations; Dialogues, including On the Nature of the Gods and On Divination; other works treating oratorical and literary subjects. Set the prose standard still followed by many of the better writers.

5. Lucretius (c. 99-55): On the Nature of Things, an exposition of Epicurean doctrines.

6. Catullus (c. 84-c. 54): Carmina (Poems) (116 extant of 120).

7. Varro (116-27), the "Encyclopedia Romana" of his age, he wrote over 600 volumes; surviving are On Farming (3 bks.), On the Latin Language (6 bks. of 25), and 600 lines of the Menippean Satires.

B. Golden (Augustan) Age, c. 40 B. C.-14 A. D.

1. Virgil (70-19 B. C.), a truly gifted poet, much memorized, quoted, and imitated: Aeneid (12 bks.); Eclogues (10 in all); Georgics (4 bks.).

2. Horace (65-8 B. C.), another poet on the "favorite author" list: Satires (2 bks.); Odes (4 bks.); Epodes; Epistles, including the Ars Poetica; Carmen Saeculare. The influence of Horace, like that of Virgil, is omnipresent in English poetry.

3. Livy (59 B. C.-17 A. D.): Ab Urbe Condita (142 bks.), a history of Rome down to his own times; 35 bks. and summaries of others survive. He believed that history afforded lessons which future generations should heed.

4. Ovid (43 B. C.-18 A. D.), an elegant and subtle poet, often imitated but seldom equalled, especially admired in the Renaissance: Amores, the moods of love; Heroides, love letters of heroines to husbands or lovers; Ars Amatoria and Remedia Amoris, "how-to" books on love; Medea, a tragedy; Metamorphoses, the single most important source of classical mythology and Ovidian views; Fasti (6 bks.), on the Roman calendar; other minor works of a more personal nature.

C. Silver Age, 1st and 2nd Centuries, A. D.

1. Valerius Maximus (fl. 14-37): Memorable Words and Deeds (9 bks.), a useful and popular compilation of anecdotes and examples.

2. Seneca the Younger (c. 4 B. C.-65 A. D.), affluent and influ-

ential member of Nero's circle, author of various treatises: Dialogues (12 in all) ; 2 moral treatises; 124 Epistles; Natural Questions (7 bks.) ; Apocolocyntosis, a satire on Claudius; Tragedies (9 or 10) , which have had wide influence in English and Italian drama: Hercules Furens (Mad Hercules) , Medea, Trojan Women, Phaedra, Agamemnon, Oedipus, Hercules Oetaeus (Hercules on Mt. Oeta) , Phoenician Women, Thyestes, and Octavia (of doubtful authorship) .

3. Lucan (39-65) : Civil War (10 bks.) , an epic treating the civil war between Pompey the Great and Caesar; left unfinished when Lucan, at Nero's request, committed suicide.

4. Statius (c. 40-c. 96) : 2 epics, Thebaid (12 bks.) and Achilleid (1 bk. and part of second written) ; Silvae (5 bks.) .

5. Valerius Flaccus (fl. c. 75) : Argonautica (8 bks., unfinished, perhaps to his credit) .

6. Pliny the Elder (24-79) , a remarkably industrious seeker after knowledge and author: Natural History (37 bks.) , all that survives of his output.

7. Juvenal (c. 60-c. 140) : Satires (16) , which became the proto-type for later writers of satire and are often quoted today.

8. Apuleius (fl. c. 155) : Metamorphoses, or Golden Ass (11 bks.) , a popular work, based on an idea of Lucian's.

9. Hyginus (pseudo-) (uncertain name of uncertain time) : Fables, a collection of myths; On Astronomy, in part mytho-logical.

CHAPTER 1

Myths of Creation and Destruction

Every society, primitive or sophisticated, is endowed with an innate curiosity about the life cycle of all living things. There is also curiosity about the apparent orderliness which can be observed and about the various natural elements, seemingly uncontrollable by man. The process of creation and destruction seems, as well, to insure a perpetuity of the universe and to suggest that super-human powers are continually operating in all kinds of life forms. Every society, therefore, has composed or inherited creation stories of the world, of man, and of powers (or gods). In time, these rationalistic myths were transferred into theological languages and metaphysical speculations.

I. Pre-Greek Myths of Creation of Universe and Man

A. Sumerian (c. 3000 B. C.)

1. First was the primeval sea, perhaps considered eternal and uncreated. Personified, the sea was the goddess, Nammu.

2. The primeval sea bore a united heaven and earth, pictured as a cosmic mountain. Personified, heaven was the male An, and earth the female Ki.

3. Heaven and earth were separated by air, the expanding element perhaps created by heaven and earth. Personified, the air-god Enlil separated An and Ki.

4. Air (or Enlil), finding himself in complete darkness, created the moon, (the god, Nanna); the moon-god then produced the sun (the god, Utu), who became brighter than his father: (note the idea of progress involved here).

5. After the separation of heaven and earth, life of every kind became possible on earth. Thus, all life may have

resulted from the union of air, earth, and water, these elements presumably assisted by the sun. Theologically, Enlil, the air-god, united with his mother Ki, the earth-goddess; of this union, with the help of Enki, the water-god, and perhaps of Utu, the sun-god, vegetable and animal life was created on earth.

6. Man was created from clay to free the gods from working for their sustenance, i.e. men are to be the servants of the gods.

7. Man, once created, was assisted by the gods, especially by Enlil (the air-god) and Enki (the sea-god). The gods gave man day, seeds, pickaxe and plow and sent down a farmer-god and a goddess of plants. Enki organized Sumeria into a civilization, decreed fates to various cities, and appointed minor deities to their duties. Enlil and Enki together dispatched a cattle-god and a grain-goddess from heaven to make earth productive in cattle and grain.

8. Enki assumed stature as the god of wisdom who dwells in the sea; he possessed all the divine decrees essential for civilization and a messenger to deliver them.

9. Heaven, as well as earth, was organized, with deities assigned special functions and abodes. Inanna was recognized as the queen of heaven, with powers comparable to those of Enki.

In passing we may note several ideas which will appear again: a son, or begotten one, who becomes stronger than the father, the begetter; the union of heaven and earth precedes all other creations; the importance of the sea-god, who becomes supreme among earth deities; light dispels darkness; there is a purpose for man's creation; civilization is bestowed upon man by the gods.

B. Babylonian (c. 1000-900 B. C.), from the Enuma Elish.

1. This myth of origins was combined with a myth of victory over disorder: Marduk, a hero chosen as champion of the older gods, overcame Tiamat, champion of the powers of darkness.

2. Man was made out of clay mixed with the flesh and blood of Tiamat, the defeated sea-monster; man was created to free the gods from working for their sustenance.

3. Portions of the monster's body were divided and became heaven and earth.

C. Hebraic, from Genesis I (not earlier than 5th century B. C.) and II (c. 8th century B. C.) .

1. On the first day, day and night were created.
2. On the second day, the firmament was created, and the waters were divided.
3. On the third day, plants were created.
4. On the fourth day, the sun and moon were created.
5. On the fifth day, marine life was created.
6. On the sixth day, animals and man were created; man, made from clay, was created to be lord of the universe.
7. The seventh day was made holy and became a day of rest.

II. Greek Cosmogonies or Theogonies

    A. Hesiod: the fullest account, it can perhaps best be seen as a genealogical chart of the early gods:

       1.

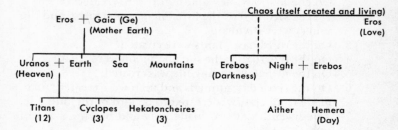

2. Kronos (Cronus), the youngest Titan, castrated his father, Uranos, with a bronze sickle given him by Earth; Kronos became ruler and married his sister, Rhea.

3. Kronos shut up the Cyclopes and Hekatoncheires (100-handed ones) in Earth, and, as Rhea bore children, he swallowed them. In this way he disposed of (temporarily) Hestia, Demeter, Hera, Hades, and Poseidon.

4. Rhea secretly hid her sixth child Zeus, and gave Kronos a stone wrapped in swaddling clothes to swallow. Zeus grew to manhood on Crete, then gave Kronos an emetic which caused him to regurgitate all that he had swallowed, last to first.

5. A ten-year struggle ensued between the children of Kronos, led by Zeus, and the Titans, led by Kronos. On Earth's advice, Zeus freed the Cyclopes and Hekatoncheires, received thunderbolts from the Cyclopes, defeated the Titans and drove them to Tartaros.

6. After the war, the sons of Kronos drew lots to determine their respective spheres of dominion: Zeus received heaven and earth. Poseidon the seas and water, and Hades the Underworld.

7. These three gods, their sisters, and their children settled on Mt. Olympus, with Zeus marrying Hera and becoming the supreme ruler. (The marriage of Zeus and Hera, called the *hieros gamos,* the "Sacred Marriage," was commemorated at Argos each year in January; similar ceremonies were held annually in several other Greek cities.)

The rather repulsive story told by Hesiod, containing both murder and cannibalism, was not of Greek origin. Most elements of his account are traceable back to Hittite and Hurrian stories, dated between 1600 and 1200 B. C.

B. Suggestions of other stories in various authors.

1. Homer says that Ocean and Tethys were the parents of all the gods.

2. Pherecydes, one of the Seven Wise Men of Ancient Greece, wrote a prose account: Chaos was first, then bore Earth, Sky, and Sea. (We have many fragments

from the 10-book work of mythology-theogony written by this 5th century B. C. author.)

3. Aristophanes in the *Birds:* Chaos and Darkness were first; Night laid an egg in Darkness, and Eros was hatched. Eros fertilized Chaos, who gave birth to Ocean, Heaven, Earth and all the gods.

4. Hyginus: Caligo (Darkness) produced Chaos; a union of these two produced Night, Day, Erebos (Underworld Darkness), and Aither. The union of Night and Erebos brought forth Death, Sleep, and many Underworld spirits. Sky and Day were parents of Earth, Heaven, and Sea; Aither and Earth produced the Titans, the Cyclopes, and the Hekatoncheires.

5. Ovid's Latin version, *Metamorphoses* 1, begins with Chaos, out of which god or nature brought order by individualizing the various elements. Following separation of the elements occurred the creation of animals—fish, wild beasts, and birds.

6. Assaults against Zeus and the Olympians:
   (a.) by the Giants, last brood of Earth (Ge) ; with aid of Heracles, the Olympians won.
   (b.) by Typhon (or Typhoeus) , a 100-headed dragon or serpent; the gods fled in terror after assuming form of various animals, but Zeus led a counter-charge which was successful.
   (c.) by Otos and Ephialtes (the Aloads) , twins who grew 9 inches every month. At the age of 9, they began to pile mountains on each other (Ossa on Pelion) to storm heaven. Zeus (or Artemis) killed them with bolts (or arrows) .

C. Creation of Man and the Role of Prometheus

1. Hesiod: no full account, but scattered statements: in *Works and Days,* gods and men have common origin, gods (Titans at the time) made the first generation of man, men of the Bronze Age were created from ash trees by Zeus.
   (a.) A somewhat detailed account of the creation of woman, Pandora, is given: Hephaistos, acting on orders of Zeus, created her from clay, with contributions given her by all the gods.

(b.) Prometheus is man's benefactor, rather than his creator.

(c.) Mankind passed through five ages: Gold (when men were blessed and blest), Silver (when Zeus ruled and became so angry that he destroyed man), Bronze (when men became fond of war, employed bronze tools and weapons), Heroes (when Theban and Trojan Wars took place and dead heroes were ruled over by Kronos in the Isles of the Blest), Iron (when men became thoroughly wicked and impious). (It may be noted that earliest accounts of a Golden Age and an Heroic Age go back to the Sumerians. In the original ideal age men had no fears and rivals, inhabited a world of peace, worshipped one god, and spoke one language (cf. Genesis 11:1-9). In the original age of heroes, three figures are dominant: Gilgamesh, Enmerkar, and Lugalbanda; the texts recounting their exploits date from 1500-1000 B. C., but the exploits may well have happened at an earlier date: in this respect, and in others, the Heroic Age and accounts of it parallel the Greek Heroic Age.)

2. Others, varying with locales: man was born of Earth herself, rose from Lake Copais, was sprung from dragon's teeth, was born from trees, or was made from stones.

(a.) Prometheus created man from clay, perhaps at Zeus' orders; Athena breathed life into the men.

(b.) Prometheus and his brother, Epimetheus, were the first mortal men.

(c.) Prometheus, a Titan, gave mankind all human arts, and, when Zeus threatened man's existence, Prometheus intervened. (For the breach between these two, read *Prometheus Bound,* by Aeschylus.) Zeus punished Prometheus directly, by having him bound to a rock in the Caucasus and visited each day by a liver-loving eagle. Zeus also punished mankind by having Pandora created, given to Epimetheus, and loosing all ills in the world. Eventually, Prometheus was freed

by Heracles, and in his honor, men began to
wear rings and wreathes. Pyrrha, daughter of
Epimetheus and Pandora, married Deucalion,
son of Prometheus; their son was Hellen, ancestor of all Greeks (Hellenes).

(d.) Ovid credited either the "maker of things" or
Prometheus with fashioning man, who was more
holy and more intelligent, made to rule other
animals, and, alone of all animals, to raise his
face toward the stars. Man then progressed
through four Ages: Gold, Silver, Bronze, and
Iron.

III. Myths of Destruction

A. Sumerian: a flood was decreed to destroy man, although
the reason is not known. Ziusudra, perhaps warned by
the water-god Enki, built a very large boat. This pious
and humble king outlasted the deluge, which raged for
7 days and 7 nights, and became himself a god, living in
Dilmun, "the place where the sun rises." (Later Babylonian and Assyrian stories, patterned closely after the
Sumerian tale, were also in circulation.)

B. Hebraic (in Genesis): all men but Noah were wicked;
Noah fashioned an ark according to God's specifications
and took on board pairs of living things. After a rain
of 40 days and 40 nights, a dove was sent out twice; on
its third mission, it didn't return. Noah disembarked and
discovered that the ark had landed on Mt. Ararat.

C. Greek: Homer told, in a simile, how Zeus had sent floods
upon wicked men; Hesiod did not mention any such
flood.

1. Apollodorus: Zeus decided to destroy Bronze Age men;
Prometheus warned his son Deucalion to build a boat
and stock it with provisions. Zeus caused a rain lasting
9 days and 9 nights, then the boat carrying Deucalion
and Pyrrha landed on Mt. Parnassus. After they made
offerings to Zeus, he, through Hermes, offered them
anything they might choose. They wanted human
company and were thereupon instructed to throw

stones behind their backs; thus, a new race was created from stone.

2. Lucian: may have known the Noah story; he said that the couple took on board their children and pairs of all animals.

3. Ovid: stories of 3 catastrophes, two floods and one fire.
   (a.) After mingling with mortals, Zeus decided to destroy wicked mankind, particularly because of the crime of Lycaon. Deucalion and Pyrrha were the only survivors and repopulated the earth by following Themis' order of throwing "the bones of their mother" (i.e. stones) behind their backs.
   (b.) Philemon and Baucis, because of their hospitality to Zeus and Hermes, survived a flood, which was apparently confined to a district of Phrygia. After many years' service as a priest and priestess, they were granted their wish of dying together: both were turned into trees, he into an oak, she into a linden.
   (c.) Another localized disaster occurred when Zeus dashed Phaëthon and the sun-chariot to earth, scorching people and lands.

4. Hyginus: combined the fire and flood catastrophes: Zeus thunderbolted Phaëthon and set the world on fire; then, on the pretext of having to put out the fire, he caused a flood and thereby destroyed mankind. Only Deucalion and Pyrrha survived the disasters.

Flood myths were common and were, therefore, subject to local variations. It is of some interest to note that the early Christians, borrowing from the fire-catastrophe tradition, believed firmly that the end of the world was near and would be destroyed by fire. The Romans, and especially Nero, quite reasonably suspected Christians' being responsible for the great fire of Rome in 64 A. D. By a reversal of roles, water, in the act of baptism, became necessary for salvation in Christian belief.

The water-and-fire theme has had a long history in literature and religious belief. Homer (*Iliad* 21) pictured the first combat between the two elements. Medieval Christianity construed Hell as a fiery place for wicked souls, but Dante in the *Inferno* neatly combined fire and ice in his concept of the place for sinners. Between Homer and Medieval Christianity was Virgil, who in *Aeneid* 6 pointed out that souls could be purified by either water or fire. Metaphysically and theologically, to these two elements mankind has always given a special significance.

Finally, two accounts of creation, based on philosophic ideas and presented by philosophers may be noted: the last part of the *Timaeus* by Plato offers a cosmology which scholars have puzzled over for many years; and, Book 5 of the *De Rerum Natura* by Lucretius gives a striking account of how man advanced from his primitive state and surroundings. Both accounts should be read by anyone interested in the origins of the world and man's progress; they reveal how far the speculative nature of man had advanced, and they show the differences between philosophic and mythological answers to the same phenomena.

CHAPTER 2
The Olympian Gods: Origins and Attributes

All authorities, from Herodotus onward, agree that Homer and Hesiod gave the Olympian gods to the Greeks. In fact, these Olympians are the featured characters in most of the Greek myths. Nor is there much doubt that these deities were introduced as objects of religious worship into Athens by the tyrant Pisistratus, who ruled from 560 to 529 B. C. Just as surely, the Olympian gods as characters in myths and as figures of worship could and did exist side by side, with little or no affinity. Although the Greeks were capable of maintaining the separation of faith and fancy, we tend to experience difficulty; for that reason, it seems appropriate to discuss the Olympians briefly as objects of worship, before presenting them as individuals in their own myths.

As distinguished from men, the gods possessed immortality, remained forever young and handsome, had power and knowledge which often seemed limitless, lived blessedly in abodes never visited by wind, rain, or snow, dined on ambrosia and nectar, and had ichor, rather than blood, flowing in their veins. Yet, their outward appearance was the same as human beings', their natures were similar to humans', and they could contract marriages with mortals. So the relationship between man and gods was both extremely close and extremely distant.

As distinguished from earlier deities, the Olympians stood in sharp contrast. The earlier, or chthonic, gods were nameless, numberless powers concerned primarily with death, mysterious and dark, worshipped at night with black-animal sacrifices, usually female and dwelling underground, often assuming vague, non-human, or animal shapes. The Olympians, on the other hand, were individualized deities, living on lofty Mt. Olympus, worshipped with white-animal sacrifices in the morning sunshine, concerned mainly with life, prayed to with hands raised and palms upward and capable of brief visits in the temples built for them. In passing, it should be emphasized that the Greeks were not idolaters who worshipped actual images which they had made. Rather, statues of the gods were created as a form of praise, just as hymns were written and sung.

As distinguished from other religions, the religion of the Greeks lacked features which many consider essential elements of any religious creed. There was no class or caste of priests, there was no dogma, there were no missions or martyrs, there was no sacred book, very little preoccupation with sin, and little regard for abject humility and blind obedience. Their religion did have, however, tenderness, humor, reverence, as well as a spirit of inquiry, a love of knowledge, and concern for life. Since it was not dogmatic, formal, and forceful, it was perhaps the most tolerant, the most truth-seeking, and the most trusting of man's abilities and intentions. For these same reasons, it was the least organized and, therefore, most subject to collapse. Before it capitulated to the more forceful religions and creeds, and this may be dated about 320 B. C., it stamped the Greeks indelibly with its glory and was stamped by them with their nobility. The Greeks did create their gods in the image of man, but they did so because of their conviction that man was the most exalted of all creatures; they were, therefore, extending the greatest compliment possible to the gods and not limiting them, as some have erroneously supposed. By such anthropomorphizing, mutual respect was established and the best possible *rapprochement* was maintained.

Let us turn now to the Olympian gods as individuals who played such a large role in the myths. Of the total number on Olympus, twelve were regarded as the major deities, united as a family headed by Zeus. Scholars differ in their opinions as to why the group was limited to twelve, but most agree that Pisistratus was in some way responsible for this particular canon: Zeus, Hera, Poseidon, Demeter, Apollo, Artemis, Ares, Aphrodite, Hermes, Athena, Hephaistos, Hestia. For the sake of convenience, we shall list the gods, indicating their Greek names, Roman equivalents, origin (where known) , attributes, spheres of influence or function, and any special items.

1. Zeus—Jupiter (or Jove): brought into Greece by the invad-

ing Achaeans, c. 1300-1200 B. C. Nilsson, in *The Mycenaean Origin of Greek Mythology*, argues that the idea of Olympus and the State of the Gods under a strong monarch had origins in the Mycenaean Age, i.e. about 1450 B. C. Attributes of Zeus included the eagle, the oak tree, lightning and thunderbolts, scepter, and throne. Zeus was the Sky and Weather; he came to be the ruler of gods and men, overlooking political and social institutions and relations. He was terrific, in the literal sense, lordly, and yet, humane; he was also considered the first god to inhabit Mt. Olympus and was, as well, the first anywhere to have games set up as an honor or praise: the Olympic games, conducted in another of Zeus' sacred precincts, were according to tradition founded in 776 B. C. The statue of Zeus for his temple in Olympia was sculptured by Phidias (5th century B. C.) and was called one of the Seven Wonders of the World. An oracle of Zeus, traditionally the oldest oracle in Greece, was located at Dodona, where Zeus spoke through the rustling of the oak leaves. At Rome, Jupiter's title, Optimus Maximus (the English translation, Best and Greatest, seems rather vapid) indicated his important position as the god of the state. His was the central position among the Capitoline Triad, and in his honor Ludi Romani (Roman Games) were celebrated each year.

2. Hera—Juno: her origin was in Argos, where, quite probably, she had early existed as a great earth-mother goddess. The story that Zeus wooed Hera for 300 years before marrying her may indicate that it took that long for the two religious concepts to syncretize. Attributes included a crown, scepter, peacock, cuckoo, and *polos* (or high headdress). She was also tall in stature, since height was requisite for beauty. As the sister-wife of Zeus, she was the goddess of marriage, married life, and the home—all of them contributing to the stability of society. Samos and Carthage were important sanctuaries for Hera. In art she was often depicted as a queenly bride, veiled, holding a scepter; a well-known statue of her was done by Polyclitus (5th century B. C.). In Homer's *Iliad* she was referred to as "ox-eyed" and "white-armed" and depicted as something of a shrew. At Rome, Juno's position was well summed up by one of her epithets, Regina (Queen). She was patroness of marriage and childbirth, and in the temple of Juno Moneta the mint was located: hence,

our word money. She was a member of the Capitoline Triad, and one of her festivals, the Matronalia, celebrated on March 1, somewhat paralleled our Mother's Day. The month of June was named in her honor and became a favorite month for marriages to be performed.

3. Poseidon—Neptune: may have had a double origin, brought in from the north by invaders c. 2000 B. C., from the east c. 1600-1200 B. C. Attributes were the trident, horse, bull, dolphin, shaggy hair and beard. He was god of all waters, horses, and earthquakes. Fine descriptions of his palace and presence occur in Homer's *Iliad* 13 and Virgil's *Aeneid* 1, respectively. Though at times bluff and gruff, he remained a very popular god. Poseidon quite possibly had originally lived as the most powerful underground deity; when he became pictured as a brother of Zeus, (younger than Zeus in Homer, but older in Hesiod), he moved to Olympus and assumed a role subsidiary to Zeus. The Isthmian games were held in his honor every four years at Corinth, and at Cape Mycale in Asia Minor the Panionia was participated in by all the Ionian Greeks of Asia Minor and the East Mediterranean islands. He was closely connected with Libya and contested for the patronage of many cities, including Athens. The latter contest, with Athena, was pictured on the west pediment of the Parthenon, and although he lost, he still was an important god to the Athenians. In art, he was shown as an athletic, bearded figure, often riding his chariot followed by mermaids or mermen.

4. Demeter—Ceres: originally known as Da-Mater (Earth-Mother) among the Achaeans, to the Athenians she was Corn-mother (or Grain-mother) and always concerned with fertility. Her attributes: sheaf of grain, tall headdress (*polos*), scepter, torch, and sacrificial bowl. The *Homeric Hymn to Demeter*, one of that collection's best poems, tells of her loss of Persephone, her subsequent search, and the founding of her mystery rites at Eleusis. The *Frogs* of Aristophanes contains a lovely choral passage describing what an initiate could hope for in his after-life. Demeter remained a favorite of country people in Greece; in Sicily, southern Italy, Asia Minor—wherever, in fact, the soil could grow barley, wheat or corn—Demeter and Persephone were worshipped. The finest statue of her, the Demeter of Cnidus, was done about 330 B. C. and now stands in the

British Museum; Leochares sculptured the head of the goddess, whose body, except for the head and forearms, is covered by a large cloak.

5. Apollo—Apollo: originally a god of Eastern peoples (particularly the Lycians) or from Northern races (especially the Dorians). His attributes are many: tripod, omphalos (= navel; it was an oval stone monument at Delphi, designating that spot as the center of the earth), lyre, bow and quiver of arrows, laurel wreath, palm tree, wolf, hawk, crow, and fawn. This list indicates the many areas of particular concern to Apollo: prophecy, medicine, the fine arts, archery, beauty, flocks and herds, law and order, courage and wisdom. The *Homeric Hymn to Apollo,* perhaps written about 700 B. C. is really two poems stitched together and reflects the fact that two sites were always associated with Apollo, the island Delos, and the holiest spot on earth, Delphi. It was common, therefore, to refer to Apollo as the Delian god or the Delphic (or Pythian) god. Though not a Greek god in origin, Apollo became the embodiment of the Hellenic spirit, the most Greek of all the gods and second only to Zeus himself. The doors on his temple at Delphi bore the inscriptions which remained the Greek models for a sane and happy life: "Know thyself" and "Nothing in excess."

It is no wonder, then, that when Rome had gained control of most of the civilized world, Augustus built a magnificent temple to Apollo in Rome, a temple, by the way, which contained the world's first public libraries. By so doing, Augustus made it clear to one and all that the center of culture and law had moved from Delphi and the Greeks to Rome and the Romans. It must be emphasized, too, that among the Greeks Apollo was *not* the god of the sun or of light; his association with the sun and light came about later when confusion resulted between his duties and those of Helios.

Apollo was a favorite subject for artists of every medium. Greek vases frequently showed him with a lyre or a bow; famous statues of him include the Apollo of Tenea (c. 525 B. C.), Apollo Sauroctonus (the Lizard-slayer), by Praxiteles (early 4th century B. C.), and the Apollo Belvedere (Hellenistic period). He also appeared on the frieze of the temple of Zeus at Olympia, skillfully represented as showing his best-known characteristic, remoteness.

6. Artemis—Diana: early considered the twin-sister of Apollo, her origin seems to have been in Asia Minor, near Ephesus; evidence shows, however, that she had counterparts in many early, Pre-Greek, sites, from the Hyperboreans in the North to the Minoans in Crete. Among her attributes are the bow and quiver of arrows, the short sleeveless hunting-dress, hair ribbon, torch, stags, deer, fish, wild goat, bear, boar, lion, wolf, horse, steer, and quail, palm tree and olive tree. Like her brother Apollo, she surveyed many things: the birth and growth of all living things, including humans, the care of wild beasts, hunting, virginity, and human femininity (but not marriage) . Her various functions may reflect her tangled origins. Many adjectives have been used to describe her: holy, pure, beautiful, enticing, remote, elusive, enchanting, irresistible, simple, brusque, wild, and cruel. Often pictured as dancing with the nymphs, she was associated with mountain heights, clear waters, springs and bright, flowery fields. The Amazons were often mentioned as her companions, and, like Apollo, her arrows brought gentle death from afar. As the "light-bearer" she roamed at night, carrying a torch; frequently, she accompanied and protected travelers. Artemis was, as well, the only Greek god to whom human sacrifices were reportedly made (e.g., Iphigenia) . Aspects of her power are illustrated by Aeschylus in *Agamemnon* and Euripides. She was the chief deity in three cities, Ephesus, Marseilles, and Syracuse. Her worship at Ephesus centered around her sacred stone (*diopet*) which had fallen from the sky; her great temple at Ephesus, rebuilt or restored by king Croesus who amassed fabulously vast wealth (mid-6th century B. C.), was classed as one of the Seven Wonders of the World. In art, Artemis was usually depicted as a tall, beautiful huntress, often accompanied by animals. Her association with the moon came later and resulted from her being identified with Hecate-Selene.

At Rome she was often called the "three-formed" goddess, i.e., Luna in the sky, Diana on earth, and Hecate in the Underworld. Altars to her were often erected at cross-roads, and several sites throughout Italy, such as Aricia, had famous shrines or temples to her.

7. Ares—Mars: originally from Thrace, his worship entered Greece by way of Macedonia and Thebes. His attributes are

war and weapons, and often he is regarded with suspicion, distrust, or hostility, even by his parents, Zeus and Hera. He was not a popular god among the Greeks, as two early stories of Homer suggest, *Iliad* 21 and *Odyssey* 8; even in Sparta he did not have great respect although there was a temple of his there. Among the Romans, Ares was early identified with Mavors (or Mars), an important agricultural deity. As father of Rome's founder, Mars was highly esteemed, having the first month of the early calendar named for him and, generally, ranking second only to Jupiter (Zeus). Ares seldom appeared in art, though, interestingly, his representations began as a bearded old man (e.g., Francois Vase) and changed to a youthful figure in helmet and armor. Both Athens and Rome had geographical spots named for Ares-Mars: in Athens, the Areopagus, the hill on which trials were held; in Rome, the Campus Martius, where elections were held, and where facilities for leisure and amusement led to its designation as the "playground of Rome."

8. Aphrodite—Venus: her origin was in the East, where she had long existed; she came to the Greeks from the Phoenicians by way of the islands of Cythera and Cyprus. Attributes included doves, apples, a mirror, attractive garments and jewelry, cosmetics, flowers and blossoms (especially roses), tamarisks, pomegranate tree, and myrtle. She was often said to have been born of sea-foam, but Homer refers to her as the daughter of Zeus and Dione. In her earliest history, she had been goddess of fertility and love; she retained these areas among the Greeks, but she also acquired others: serene seas and ocean travel, nature in bloom, and charm. She could, however, be cruel to those who doubted or flouted her power, as many plays of Euripides and many stories in Ovid's *Metamorphoses* attest. Aphrodite represented, above all else, sexual love and desire, but among the Greeks, sex, like all pleasures, had to be enjoyed in moderation. The leering attitude of today would not have been tolerated by the Greeks, who had a much more sensible and well-balanced outlook. Common epithets of her were "golden" and "smiling," and, as Hesiod observed, to her belong "girlish babble and deceit, sweet rapture, embraces and caresses." The *Homeric Hymn to Aphrodite* speaks of her arrival in Cyprus, where she was welcomed and joyfully dressed and adorned by the Hours. The Graces were often associated with

her, and a reference in *Jeremiah* refers to her as the "queen of heaven." Special sites of her worship were Paphos (in Cyprus), Corinth, and Eryx (in Western Sicily). In Orphic belief, e.g., Empedocles, Aphrodite came to symbolize the unifying force in the universe, and in Athens, her epithet Pandemos (of all the people), represented a political ideal. In art, Aphrodite appeared, from early days, as a nude standing goddess (the only goddess depicted so), or a draped, seated figure holding a dove. In the 5th century B. C., she was often dressed in transparent clothing, but in the 4th century B. C., Praxiteles created a sensation by sculpturing her naked. This work, called the Aphrodite of Cnidus was praised for centuries, and by connoisseurs such as Pliny the Elder (*Natural History* 36.20 ff.). Of almost equal fame today is the Aphrodite from Melos (Venus de Milo), dated in the 2nd century B. C. Found on the isle of Melos in 1820, the goddess stands 6'8" but still is the personification of physical perfection.

Among the Romans Venus held an honored position, since the whole Roman race derived from her son Aeneas. Julius Caesar claimed direct descendency from her through Julus, son of Aeneas and he built in her honor the temple of Venus Genetrix (Mother), dedicated in 46 B. C. There is a beautiful hymn to Venus by Lucretius, at the opening of his *De Rerum Natura*. Finally, the largest temple built in ancient Rome was the temple of Venus and Roma, erected in the reign of Hadrian (117-138 A. D.)

9. Hermes—Mercury: his origin goes back to the meaning of his name, "stone-heap;" among the Pre-Hellenic peoples of Greece, this was probably not his name, but heaps of stones were used as landmarks in primitive times. Attributes include a hat (often broad-rimmed and with wings, the *petasus*), herald's staff (*caduceus*), winged sandals (*talaria*), a ram, lyre, and shepherd's staff. Tradition called him the son of Zeus and Maia and placed his birth on Mt. Cyllene. Hermes had many functions, as befitted such a ubiquitous and agile deity: protector of shepherds and flocks, guide and protector of travelers, conductor of the souls of the dead, a messenger of Zeus (in the *Odyssey,* but not so in the *Iliad*), bringer of good luck, patron of orators, writers, athletes, merchants and thieves. His many epithets stress his ingenuity, speed and protectiveness. He was

perhaps the most loved of the Olympians, even though he was not considered one of the mightier gods. Yet he had interests everywhere—in the country, in the cities, in daytime or at night. Perhaps he, more than any other god, constantly reminded man that this is a capricious world. The *Homeric Hymn to Hermes* (c. 600 B. C.) tells of his adventures shortly after birth; among these were his theft of big-brother Apollo's cattle and the invention of the 7-string lyre, making use of a tortoise shell. In the *Homeric Hymn to Demeter,* Hermes leads Persephone up from the dead, leads Eurydice up and back, and leads Protesilaus up for his three-hour visit on earth: his conducting of souls led to his epithet *psychopompos.* Homer had him lead King Priam through the Greek lines to the tent of Achilles, there to reclaim Hector's body (*Iliad* 24). Hermes was also referred to by authors as "cleverest of the gods," "friendliest of the gods to men," "Argus-slayer," and one who could "slip into a room like a breeze through a keyhole." In earlier art, Hermes was depicted as an older, bearded guide, but his association with athletics and the gymnasia changed him into a young, athletic type. Recalling the picture of him given by Virgil in *Aeneid* 4, one can readily understand his appearance today as the patron of F.T.D. (Floral Telegraph Delivery).

10. Athena—Minerva: her origin was two-fold: as a palace-goddess among the Minoans (c. 1900-c. 1500 B. C.), to whom she may have been known as the protector-warrior aspect of the Earth-mother goddess; and, as the skilled and wise patroness of Athens. The question of which gave its name to which, the city to the goddess or the goddess to the city, is as unanswerable as the chicken-and-egg question. Her attributes, many from her olden days, were a shield, snake, tree, bird, owl, lamp, helmet, Nike (Victory), and olive (tree and oil); it was said that she was born full-grown from the head of Zeus, without the aid of a woman as mother; another version, often followed by artists, said that Hephaistos or Prometheus or Hermes split Zeus' head with an axe, and out leaped Athena. Her concerns were war, wisdom, arts and crafts, unmarried girls, justice, and most of all, Athens. It was Pisistratus, the famous patron of art, who linked the goddess and the city together in a bond which lasted for almost 900 years. There was a striking masculinity about Athena, not found in any other goddess, probably be-

cause of her unusual and unnatural birth; noticeably, she was the protectress and helper of Odysseus, Perseus, and Bellerophon. Homer refers to her often as "grey-eyed" or "owl-eyed," and in the *Eumenides* of Aeschylus, she casts a deciding vote, creating the world's first hung jury. As patroness of Athens, her image was often engraved on coins (which showed an owl on the reverse side), and there were fine statues and temples of her. Phidias, for example, created the Athena Promachos (Defender) and the masterful Athena Parthenos (Virgin); the Athena of Lemnos was simply referred to as "the Beautiful." The Parthenon was, of course, her best and most famous temple; its pedimental sculptures included the scene of her birth and her contest with Poseidon for patronage of Athens. The frieze on the *cella* of the Parthenon showed Athenians in the Panathenaic procession, part of the biennial and quadrennial festival in her honor. She was, as another of her epithets said, Polias, "of the city." Among the early Romans, she became identified with Minerva, who, along with Jupiter (Zeus) and Juno (Hera) composed the Capitoline Triad of gods. Most representations of Athena pictured her with helmet on, bearing (or near) her aegis (on which was fastened the head of Medusa), carrying or holding a spear, accompanied by a small Nike (goddess of Victory). As Cook and Seltman have pointed out, the goddess of pagan Athens very easily became the Virgin Mary of Athens, as the titles show: Pallas Athene Parthenos Gorgo Epekoos ("Maiden Athena, Virgin, Terrible, Hearkening-to-prayer") was replaced by Mater Theou Parthenos Athenaia Gorgo Epekoos ("Mother of God, Virgin Athenian One, Terrible, Hearkening-to-prayer").

At Rome, Minerva was especially popular with women, poets and artists, and all artisans. Appropriately, a statue of Minerva stands in the library of Yale's College of Architecture.

11. Hephaistos (Hephaestus) —Vulcan (or Mulciber): His origin was single, in the Bronze Age of Greece (c. 1200-1100 B. C.) traceable from Lycia (in Asia Minor), to Lemnos, and thence to Athens. His attributes were hammer, anvil, bellows, fire, forge, and lameness. He served as an artisan-god, a skilled worker in metals; he was, in fact, the only Olympian pictured by Homer as consistently at work. One tradition referred to him as the son of Zeus and Hera but it was more commonly believed

that Hera bore him without the aid of a male. It has been suggested, as well, that his importance might have been stressed
by his being lame, that is, he was incapable of running away.
His lameness resulted from his being thrown to earth by Zeus or
by Hera, or so the stories said. Homer may have simply thought,
or noticed, that a smith working at his anvil naturally developed powerful arm, chest, and shoulder muscles, thus making
his legs seem weak. The greatest work of Hephaistos in the *Iliad*
was, of course, the marvelous armor for Achilles, sought by
Thetis and wrought by the god because of her earlier kindnesses
to him. In the *Aeneid,* similar armor is made by Vulcan for
Aeneas. From the 4th century B. C. on, Hephaistos' popularity
waned, as less and less respect was given him; the amazing jet-
gas emanating from Mother-earth in Lycia shrank to the fire
belched out by a volcano in Roman days. A temple for Hephaistos was erected in Athens between 450 and 440 B. C.; it stands
today as the best preserved of the Greek temples, yet for many
years it was called the Theseum (by an irony of fate). Today,
Hephaistos may have gained new stature, or at least a measure
of revenge, and a return to his original meaning; for, in *Iliad*
18 Homer says: "He (Hephaistos) was making a set of twenty
three-legged tables to stand round the walls of his well-built
halls. He had fitted golden wheels to all their legs, so that they
could run by themselves to a meeting of the gods and amaze
the company by running home again ..." (translation by E. V.
Rieu). Perhaps Homer was wiser than we have thought, prophe-
cying automatic automobiles run by gas?

At Rome, Vulcan's sacred precinct was outside the city walls;
we read or hear little about him, except for the wonderful
armor he fashions for Aeneas in Book 8 of the *Aeneid.* A statue
of him now stands in Birmingham, Alabama, which calls itself
the "Pittsburgh of the South."

12. Hestia—Vesta: the "Cinderella" of the Olympians, she
tended the hearth-fire of the Olympian family and stayed at
home when they went out. She was recognized as the important
goddess of the hearth, whether it be a family, community, or
godly hearth. Tradition regarded her as the first child of Kronos
and Rhea, thus making her the oldest and most sacred of the
Olympians. Her role in mythology was almost non-existent,
and, when it became evident that Dionysos would have to be

counted among the "Big Twelve," it was Hestia who quietly stepped aside. She did, however, have to remain as an Olympian to keep the fire alive. In Rome, her temple was a well-known round temple, with a shrine which only the Vestal Virgins could enter. Vestals were six in number and were selected when they were between the ages of 6 and 10; the normal tour of duty was 30 years, after which they retired and could marry (though most didn't) . Punishment for allowing the sacred fire to go out was scourging, for unchastity, burial alive. Guides in Rome will show you the place where unchaste Vestals were so entombed.

With Hestia we conclude our "snapshots" of the Twelve Olympian gods. Their escapades in myths will follow, and hopefully, will mean more now that each deity is recognizable as an individual. For more comprehensive treatments of the gods, these books are particularly valuable: W. K. C. Guthrie, *The Greeks and Their Gods;* Walter F. Otto, *The Homeric Gods;* Charles Seltman, *The Twelve Olympians;* Martin P. Nilsson, *The Mycenaean Origin of Greek Mythology* and *Greek Folk Religion;* Jane Harrison, *Mythology;* and, H. J. Rose, *A Handbook of Greek Mythology* and *Gods and Heroes of the Greeks.* (All are available in paper-back editions and will lead those interested in further study to such important works as those of Farnell, Cook, and Wilamowitz.)

CHAPTER 3

The Lesser Olympians and Other Gods

In this section we shall consider first, the gods who lived on Olympus but were not members of the official "family," and secondly, other (or non-Olympus-dwelling) Greek and Roman gods and goddesses.

A. Inhabitants of Olympus

1. Dionysos—Bacchus, Liber: his origins were in Thrace and Phrygia, and his route into Greece was through Macedonia and Thessaly into Thebes, Delphi, Athens, Corinth, and other centers. His attributes included grapevine, ivy, grapes, thyrsos (a staff wrapped in vines and topped with a pinecone), drinking-cup, leopard, fawn, deer, Silenoi, Pans, Satyrs, Bacchantes, ecstasy, enthusiasm, fawn-skin shirt, drama (both tragedy and comedy), and mysticism. His functions embraced cultivation of wine and wine-making, concern for vegetable life and fertility, and patronage of poetry, drama and song. The *Homeric Hymn of Dionysos* (c. 700 B. C.) told of his capture by Tyrsenian pirates and his escaping his bonds, turning the ship's mast into a grape-vine and the men into dolphins; the subject was popular among artists, and one of our finest treasures from antiquity is the drinking bowl painting of this scene by Exekias (c. 540 B. C., and now in Munich). Homer certainly knew Dionysos as a god but not one of the Twelve Olympians; the *Bacchae,* a play by Euripides, illustrates several aspects of the advent and worship of Dionysos: hostility shown him by a king, his epiphany to the king and gradual takeover of the king's mind and will, the excesses of his worshippers (especially the female Maenads) and how they experi-

enced both ecstasy and enthusiasm, and the final fulfillment of their devotion by eating flesh and drinking
blood of an animal representing the god himself. The
strange, mystic powers of Dionysos, and the wild mountain and woodland revels in his honor were entirely un-
Greek, and yet, in time, his worship was so well combined with that of other gods that he could share
Apollo's shrine at Delphi. So popular did he become
that by 432 B. C. he had displaced the quiet Hestia as
one of the twelve major Olympians. His worship was
introduced at Corinth by the tyrant Periander (c. 625-
585 B. C.), at Sicyon (and perhaps at Delphi) by Cleis-
thenes, at Athens by Pisistratus. The Greater Dionysia,
celebrated in March, and the Lesser Dionysia, celebrated
in December, were times of joy and merry-making in the
city and country, respectively; dramatic performances
were staged in his honor during the Greater Dionysia.
In 186 B. C., the Roman Senate issued its Decree Concerning Bacchanals, one of our earliest surviving Roman
inscriptions. One of his festivals in Rome, the Liberalia,
occurred on March 17; and, on this date, boys became
citizens by putting on the *toga virilis* (toga of manhood). His Roman name of Liber meant "free," and so
Dionysos was "The Free-er," for good or bad. A few
mortals, notably Alexander the Great and Mark Antony,
compared themselves to Dionysos—obviously, both were
possessed by the god at the time. In art, he was at first
pictured as bearded and wearing flowing garments; later,
a youthful, beardless type emerged and was often given
soft, effeminate features. Frequently, as in the fine mosaic
on Delos, he is accompanied by leopards or riding in a
chariot drawn by leopards. (It must be abundantly
clear at point that his inclusion among the "Lesser Olympians" rests solely on the fact that he was not originally
one of the divine canon of 12).

2. Persephone (or Kore)—Proserpina: her attributes and
    functions are inextricably bound up with those of her
    mother Demeter. There is a fine artistic representation
    of her, in the company of Demeter and Triptolemos,
    from Eleusis, where she was an integral figure in the

mystery-rites. She was also depicted as wife of Hades (Pluto) and queen of the Lower World.

3. Iris—Iris: she served as messenger of the gods, especially of Zeus and Hera and had, therefore, the necessary wings and staff.

4. Hebe—Hebe: known for two attributes, as cup-bearer for the gods and as goddess of youthfulness; she became the wife of Heracles after his deification.

5. Eros—Cupid (or Amor) : associated with Aphrodite at an early date, he came to be regarded as her son, sharing her concern for love and fertility, her power among men and gods, and her role as a philosophic cosmic force. (See, for example, his functions in Ovid's *Metamorphoses*). Virgil depicts him in delightful fashion in *Aeneid* 1; in art, he is usually wearing wings, wearing a quiver of arrows, carrying his trusty bow, and looking cherubic.

6. Heracles—Hercules: since his full story will be presented later, here it will suffice to say that, by his courageous deeds, he won his way to Olympus, where he settled down as the husband of Hebe.

7. Asklepios—Aesculapius: had a two-fold origin, one in Thessaly where he became more of a hero than a god, the other in Epidaurus (in Argos) where he became a god after being killed by a thunderbolt of Zeus. His attribute was the staff with a serpent, later two serpents, twined around it, and his only concern was with medicine. Epidaurus was the center of his worship, and from that city he was introduced into Athens in 420 B. C. Sophocles was said to have entertained him in his home, and Aristophanes, in the *Plutus,* describes the procedure for curing ills. The second most important site for the cult and healing was the island Cos, which was the home of the famous practitioner, Hippocrates. Asklepios was brought to Rome in the early 3rd century B. C., and his shrine and sanitarium were established on the island in the center of the Tiber River. That the island is still the site of a hospital testifies to the efficacy of the spot as a place for healing.

B. Other (non-Olympian) Greek gods

1. Helios—Sol (or Phoebus) : son of Hyperion and Theia, this brother of Selene and Eos served as the sun-god. Each day he drove his chariot up out of the Ocean, across the sky, and into the Ocean. From his vantage point, he could see everything that happened on earth, and so he was often thought to be all-knowing, as well. A special site of his worship was the island of Rhodes, where there stood a statue of Helios, created by Chares. Called the Colossus of Rhodes, it was one of the Seven Wonders of the World, erected c. 290 B. C., and destroyed by earthquake in 225 B. C. Among the Romans, he was referred to frequently as Sol Invictus (the Unconquerable Sun), perhaps because of the worship of Mithra or Baal as a sun-god. Helios became totally confused with Apollo, never a sun-god to the Greeks.

2. Selene—Luna: sister of Helios and Eos, she was the moon-goddess, whose chariot was drawn by horses or cows. Since the crescent of the moon resembles cow's horns, she was sometimes depicted as having horns on her brow. Selene later was identified with Artemis, then among the Romans, with Diana who was often called the "three-formed goddess," i.e., Luna in the sky, Diana on earth, and Hecate in the Lower World. (It may also be safe to report that no students of selenography have as yet turned into lunatics.)

3. Eos—Aurora: sister of Helios and Selene she was the goddess of dawn; her long-standing epithet was "rosy-fingered," and it was her task to fly through the eastern sky in her winged chariot to herald the coming of Helios. In turn, her coming was heralded by Phosphoros (or Hesperos) —Lucifer, the morning star.

4. Charites—Gratiae—the Graces: originally two in number, they were increased to three and personified grace and beauty. Their names were Aglaea (Brilliance), Euphrosyne (Mirth), and Thalia (Bloom) ; frequently they accompanied Aphrodite. They were worshipped widely throughout Greece but had no cult in Rome.

5. Muses: starting as a single Muse, the group increased to 9, and beginning as fountain nymphs, they developed

into individual patrons of arts and sciences. Tradition calls their parents Zeus and Mnemosyne (Memory) and says their favorite haunts were: Mt. Helicon, especially the springs, Aganippe and Hippocrene, located at the foot of Helicon, Pieria (in Thrace), Delphi, and Mt. Parnassus. Their names and special interests: Calliope (epic poetry), Clio (history), Erato (lyric and love poetry), Euterpe (music and flute-playing), Melpomene (tragedy), Polyhymnia (sacred song), Terpsichore (dance), Thalia (comedy), and Urania (astronomy).

6. Horae (Hours) : at first two in number, they increased to four in order to correspond to the four seasons. Hesiod considered them as three daughters of Zeus and Themis, named Dike (Justice), Eunomia (Good Order), and Eirene (Peace); he listed their functions as guardians of agriculture and of social and political order. To Homer, the Horae guarded the gates of heaven, controlled the weather, and presided over the changes of seasons and the accompanying growth and decay of nature. The Athenians worshipped two Horae, Thallo (Blossom, goddess of spring flowers) and Carpo (Ripeness, goddess of summer fruits).

7. Morpheus: son of Hypnos (Sleep), he was the god of dreams. He appeared in human form and voice in peoples' dreams. In later tradition, because of literary allusions, he was referred to as the god of sleep.

8. Moirae—Parcae: more powerful than the Olympian gods themselves, these three goddesses were identified as the Fates. Homer speaks of a single Moira and plural Moirae and gives their parents as Night and Darkness, and Zeus and Themis. Hesiod represented them as Clotho (the spinner), Lachesis (disposer of lots), and Atropos (the inevitable) ; Clotho spins of the thread of life, Lachesis measures it, and Atropos cuts it. Their duty was to see that each person's fate, assigned at birth, was carried out. In art, they appear without attributes (e.g. on the Francois Vase), or with a spindle, scroll, and scissors (or pair of scales).

9. Nemesis: daughter of Nyx and Erebos (Night and Darkness), she was regarded the goddess of law and justice,

the personification of avenging retribution who particularly sought out those guilty of the sin of presumption. Her most famous shrine was at Rhamnus (in Attica), where two temples were built for her (c. 490 B. C., and c. 436 B. C.; the latter was never completed) ; her statue at Rhamnus was sculptured by Agoracritus, a pupil of the master Phidias. Artists presented her as winged or borne in a chariot drawn by griffins, holding a pair of scales, whip, sword, apple bough, or wheel (of fortune) .

10. Themis—Justitia: daughter of Gaia and Uranos, a prophetic goddess of law, justice, and order, and a patroness of the rights of hospitality. Her oracle at Delphi was later taken over by Apollo; it was she who instructed Deucalion and Pyrrha and gave prophecies to Prometheus, Poseidon, and Zeus. Athens, Delphi, Olympia and Thebes were special sites of her worship.

11. Hymen or Hymenaeus: a personified marriage song or chant, he was artistically portrayed as a young man carrying a torch. Later tradition referred to him as a son of Apollo and one of the Muses.

12. Sea Deities: the roles of some of these will be considered in the Myths of the Sea (Chapter 6) .

    (a.) The Halioi Gerontes (Old Men of the Sea) : Proteus, Nereus, Glaucus, Phorcys, Thaumas.

    (b.) Leukothea and Palaimon, both of whom were mortals changed to sea deities; Palaimon had his own temple in Corinth and, in time, became identified with the Roman god of ports, Portunus.

    (c.) Nereids: 50 daughters of Nereus and Doris, the most famous of which were Amphitrite (wife of Poseidon), Thetis (wife of Peleus and mother of Achilles) , and Galatea (loved by Polyphemos) . They often accompanied Poseidon and were imagined as beautiful maidens singing, dancing, and playing instruments or riding along the sea on the backs of sea-creatures. They were helpful to voyagers and aided mariners in distress; hence, they were mainly worshipped on islands, along coasts, and at the mouths of rivers. Hesiod was the first author to list all 50 names (*Theogony*) .

    (d.) Oceanus and Tethys: husband and wife, they lived

in the western-most part of the world, never concerning themselves with affairs on Olympus. They were the parents of 3,000 sons, who became gods of all the world's rivers, and of 3,000 daughters, nymphs of the ocean and rivers. (The latter were called Oceanids.)

(e.) Sirens: sea-nymphs who by their beautiful singing, lured sailors to their deaths. In origin they were young maids, companions of Persephone, possessed with lovely voices. Upon the abduction of Persephone by Hades, the Sirens prayed that they be given wings to aid in the search; thus, they became half-birds and half-women. Homer mentioned two Sirens; three were often imagined; usually, however, they are thought of as a large group. Two voyagers who managed to sail past the Sirens were Odysseus and Jason.

(f.) Gorgons: three daughters of Phorcys and Ceto, they were beautiful maidens who were transformed into ugly monstrous beings with serpents for hair, claws of bronze, and staring eyes capable of turning anyone who looked at them into stone. Named Stheno, Euryale, and Medusa, they lived in the Western Ocean. Medusa, the only mortal Gorgon, was killed by Perseus. Greek artists had great fun portraying them, since so much imagination could be employed in the task.

(g.) Harpies: two or three or several daughters of Thaumas and Electra, they were winged monsters, part woman and part bird, who were always filthy and hungry. They sometimes acted as divine avengers of justice, sometimes punished criminals themselves. Their name means "Snatchers," and they were most often portrayed as snatchers of food from the living or snatchers of souls of the dead. Quite likely, their origin lay in the storm-winds and squalls at sea. Homer names only one (Podarge), but three were often named: Aello, Ocypete, Celaeno; occasionally, others are mentioned.

(h.) Scylla and Charybdis: twin terrors of sailors, their stories will be told later in the Myths of the Sea.

(i.) Tritons: male counterparts to the Nereids, the Tritons were mermen who usually accompanied Poseidon but sometimes pursued Nereids. Their common attribute was a shell-trumpet with which waves could be stirred up or calmed.

13. Earth Deities: only occasionally does any of their number figure in a myth.

(a.) Naiads: female nymphs who presided over springs, fountains, streams, and rivers. They were imagined as beautiful girls, with their heads crowned with flowers, light-hearted, gay, and kind to humans.

(b.) Dryads (or Hamadryads) : wood nymphs attached to trees, they lived and died with their trees, sharing the tree's fortunes, good or bad.

(c.) Oreads: nymphs of the mountains, most commonly associated with Artemis, and therefore, specially honored by hunters.

(d.) Minor male spirits: satyrs or Silenoi, horse-men or goat-men who walked on two legs; Centaurs, who walked on four legs, and included some famous names (Chiron and Nessus, for example); Curetes, Cretan attendants of Zeus who drowned out the infant Zeus' cries by their dancing and clashing of shields and spears; Corybantes, often wrongly equated with Curetes, were attendants of Cybele, the Phrygian Earth-mother goddess.

(e.) Pan: goat-man who haunted the forests, often playing his pipes; he enjoys the distinction of having had more English poems written to or about him than any other mythological character, even though he appeared seldom in Greek myths. He was at home in Arcadia, from which place his worship spread to all parts of Greece in the early 5th century B. C. Sudden terror (panic) without reasonable or visible cause was ascribed to his influence. Athenians built a cave-shrine to Pan on the Acropolis and held annual sacrifices and torch-races in his honor. His death was the only god's death announced and was described by Plutarch. The Romans identified him with Faunus.

(f.) Chloris—Flora: goddess of spring and flowers, wife of Zephyros (Zephyr), the West Wind. Her festival at Rome, called the Floralia, was the precursor of our May-day festivals.

(g.) Aeolus: king of the winds who kept his chargers pent up in a mountain in Aeolia. A fine picture of him and his duties is given by Virgil in *Aeneid* 1.

(h.) Winds: though many more were recognized, four were generally named: Eurus (East Wind), Zephyros (West Wind), Boreas (North Wind), and Notus (South Wind). Traditionally these four were brothers.

(i.) Priapus: a promoter of fertility in crops, animals, and humans. Statues of him were frequently set up in gardens and vineyards, and the first fruits of gardens and fields were regularly sacrificed to him. Romans identified him with Mutinus, another fertility god.

C. Roman Deities: there is little mythology concerning these figures.

1. Saturn: an old god of agriculture, he became identified with the Greek Kronos. He and his wife Ops were the parents of Picus. An ancient temple to Saturn near the Capitoline Hill housed the state treasury. A week-long festival, the Saturnalia, was celebrated each year in December; in many respects, it preceded our Christmas and New Year festivities, with December 25 being the height of the "season." He was subsequently honored by having a planet and a day named for him.

2. Janus: an ancient god of doorways who became the patron of all undertakings and god of all beginnings. He was credited with having given the Romans knowledge of law and coinage, and his image was the most popular one used on coins. He was a god one could never miss or forget, since he had two faces (appropriate to the god of doorways). When the calendar was expanded, the new first month was named in his honor. His name was the first invoked in prayers, and he received the first part of every sacrifice. His temple in Rome served as a sort of armory; its doors were open in time of war, closed in

time of peace. His chief festival occurred on January 9, and finally, the highest of Rome's seven hills, the Janiculum, was named for him.

3. Faunus: old Italian god of forests and wild life, a fertility spirit who became identified with the Greek Pan. An early legend described him as the grandson of Saturn and son of Picus, king of Latium, and father of Latinus (who became Aeneas' father-in-law). Two annual festivals honored him, in December and February, with libations of milk and wine, sacrifices of goats, and games. He was sometimes associated with Bona Dea.

4. Juturna: a Roman goddess of springs, given immortality by Jupiter after admitting him to her embraces. There was a pool sacred to her in the Roman Forum. In Virgil's *Aeneid*, she is sent by Juno to stir up the Latins to break an oath.

5. Silvanus: ancient Roman god of land lying outside recognized boundaries. He was feared, and was propitiated every time new ground was broken or new land cleared. He was sometimes identified with Pan or Faunus.

6. Vertumnus and Pomona: god of gardens and goddess of orchards, they had a love affair of sorts: in various disguise, he tried to woo and win her but to no avail. As soon as he resumed his true shape, however, she fell in love with him, and they happily tended their gardens together thereafter.

7. Mater Matuta: originally the goddess of dawn, she assumed the duties of protectress of women in childbirth and of seas and harbors. She was sometimes identified with Leucothea, and her feast occurred each year on June 11.

8. Quirinus: was the deified founder of Rome, Romulus; he was accorded a separate college of priests, an honor given only to Jupiter and Mars.

9. Lucina: goddess of child-birth, frequently listed as one aspect of Diana; (see Virgil, *Eclogue* 4).

10. Household gods: Lares, guardians of the home, protectors of travelers on land and on sea; Penates, guardians of the storeroom, honored at every hearth, first brought to Italy from Troy by Aeneas; Manes, spirits of the dead, honored by festivals in February.

11. Concordia: goddess of harmony, a temple was established to her in 367 B. C., after the Licinian-Sextion Laws were passed. The Senate often met in her temple.

12. Pales: an ancient god of flocks and shepherds, he was honored by having the Palatine hill named for him.

13. Consus: ancient god of the safely harvested grain, his temple stood on the Aventine Hill, and his festival was held August 21. The mule was sacred to him.

14. Bellona: goddess of war who accompanied Mars into combat; her shrine on the Capitoline Hill was destroyed by fire in 48 B. C.

15. Terminus: god who protected boundaries; February 23 was his holiday. Legend said that he was a native inhabitant of the Capitoline Hill and did not yield with the advent of Jupiter to the Capitoline.

16. Roma: the personification of the city of Rome, where all roads led. The largest temple ever built was to Venus and Roma, erected (and perhaps designed) by Hadrian, in the 2nd century A. D.

Though these lists are not exhaustive, the number of deities named and their particular spheres of habitation and influence will, it is hoped, indicate the infinite variety of gods worshipped by people of all ranks. The Romans carried the idea to a logical conclusion by believing that every person had a sort of god, or guardian angel, looking after him and his affairs. This guiding spirit, called the *genius,* was later applied to the whole state of Rome, so that a corporate community was achieved; in time, the emperor, who physically represented the state, had his genius regarded as an object of worship, especially in the Eastern areas. Thus, a spiritual one-worldness came into being and was partly responsible for the success of the Roman Empire. Still, the older Italian and Greek-turned-Roman deities retained some followers and respect until they capitulated before Christianity.

CHAPTER 4

Loves, Quarrels and Battles of the Gods

A. Love Stories (or, "A funny thing happened on the way to . . .").

Some comments should perhaps precede the many tales of love recounted below: (1.) The three most powerful gods—Zeus, Poseidon, Apollo—are the most active in these stories. This fact is undoubtedly to be explained as the process of religious syncretizing at work; as foreign male deities, they had to be reconciled to the existing, older female deities, and such accommodation was easily managed by creating love stories. (2.) The notion that gods assumed animal or bird forms in many of these episodes harks back to the pre-Olympian religion, when gods were incarnate in certain birds and animals. (3.) The concept of the "Sacred Marriage" probably lay behind the composition of many of the stories: Zeus, especially, as the sky-god, mated with women representing the earth-goddess. (4.) Some of the stories were clearly eponymous: people of different racial extraction and in different regions invented stories involving a god (particularly Zeus) in order to enhance their own prestige and pride. (5.) Although there are occasional references to other Olympians' marriages, only in the case of Zeus and Hera was a full marriage-rite solemnized and reported.

Zeus: the number of his affairs—we know of over 50—stretched Hera's patience to the breaking point, but since she could not harm Zeus, she frequently unleashed her wrath against his loves and/or the offspring of these amours. Yet Hera herself was the last of a succession of wives of Zeus; how many such affairs Zeus engaged in while married to an earlier wife we do not hear of. It was only Hera who became the traditionally wronged wife, and this might be credited to Homer's treatment of the royal pair. Hesiod (*Theogony*) listed these wives and children of Zeus:

1. Metis (Wisdom) : Athena (Zeus swallowed both Metis and unborn Athena to prevent the birth of any child of Metis).
2. Themis (Law) : Horai (Hours), Moirai (Fates).
3. Eurynome (Wide-ruling), an Oceanid: Charites (Graces).
4. Demeter (Earth-mother) : Persephone.
5. Mnemosyne (Memory) : Muses.
6. Leto (Woman?), a Titaness: Apollo and Artemis. (Another tradition says that both Leto and Zeus took the form of quail in this affair.)
7. Hera (Lady) : Ares, Hebe, Eileithyia, Hephaistos.

Dione, not mentioned by Hesiod, was the mother of Aphrodite as related by Homer (*Iliad* 5). Maia, the oldest of the Pleiades and the mother of Hermes, was sometimes considered a wife of Zeus.

Of Zeus' other affairs, the following list will suffice to show the variety of epiphanies by Zeus and the offspring, some of whom became eponyms, others of whom became renowned heroes.

Love	Form taken by Zeus	Offspring
1. Europa	1. white bull	1. Minos and Rhadamanthus
2. Io	2. dark cloud	2. Epaphos
3. Callisto	3. Artemis	3. Arcas
4. Antiope	4. satyr	4. Amphion and Zethus
5. Danaë	5. shower of gold	5. Perseus
6. Leda	6. swan	6. Helen and Polydeuces (Pollux)
7. Aegina	7. flame of fire (?)	7. Aeacus
8. Electra	8. himself, without majesty	8. Dardanus
9. Laodamia	9. himself, without majesty	9. Sarpedon
10. Niobe	10. himself, without majesty	10. Argus and Pelasgus
11. Semele	11. himself, without majesty	11. Dionysos
12. Alcmena	12. Amphitryon	12. Heracles

Comments: According to tradition, Niobe was the first mortal lover, and Alcmena the last mortal lover, of Zeus.

Semele, tricked by Hera, managed to have Zeus appear in all his majesty; as a result, she died, and Zeus carried Dionysos in his thigh until time for his birth.

The children of these unions were associated with every region of the ancient world: Minos and Rhadamanthus became kings of Crete, and, along with Aeacus, judges of the Lower World; Epaphos became a king in Egypt; Arcas was the ancestor of all Arcadians, as Argus was of all Argives and Pelasgus of all Pelasgians; Amphion and Zethus were associated closely with Thebes; Dardanus became the ancestor of the Trojans: Helen was associated variously with Sparta, Troy, and Egypt, while Polydeuces took part in the Argonauts' expedition and became a hero at Sparta; another hero, Perseus, had adventures over most of the world, as did the two who became gods, Dionysos and Heracles; Homer recounts the death of Sarpedon, king of Lycia and ally of Troy *(Iliad* 16) . Thus, these loves and their offspring represent the universality of Zeus, the syncretizing process at work, and the fact that every city, race, and hamlet wished to show some link to the "father of gods and men."

Zeus figured in one story of homosexual love: having spied on the handsome Trojan prince, Ganymede, Zeus, perhaps in the form of an eagle, carried him off to Olympus to become the cupbearer of the gods.

Finally, one tradition had it that Zeus assumed the form of a cuckoo to win Hera's love, then resumed his true shape, married her and spent a wedding night on Samos lasting for 300 years.

Poseidon: his traditional wife was Amphitrite, a Nereid, who, like her sister-in-law, Hera, had to put with a lecherous husband. The element of violence entered some of Poseidon's love stories and some of the offspring of these unions proved to be violent characters. By Amphitrite, Poseidon became father of Triton, Rhode, and Benthesicyme. Except as noted, Poseidon appeared as himself in these stories.

Love	Offspring
1. Medusa	1. Pegasus and Chrysaor
2. Demeter: (both assumed forms of horses)	2. Arion (a swift horse) and Despoena
3. Tyro: (as river-god Enipeus)	3. Neleus and Pelias
4. Amymone	4. Nauplius
5. Scylla	5. None: (Amphitrite turned her into a monster)
6. Gaia	6. Antaeus
7. Hippothoë	7. Taphios
8. Thoossa	8. Polyphemus

Love	Offspring
9. Celaeno, a Pleiad	9. Lycus and Nyctaeus
10. Chione	10. Eumolpus
11. Libya	11. Agenor and Belus
12. Theophane: (she had assumed form of sheep, so he became a ram)	12. ram with golden fleece for which Jason sailed
13. Alope	13. Hippothous

Comments: Again, this is not a complete file on the affairs of a god. Two other episodes of note were these: an affair with Aphrodite, who bore Poseidon Rhodus and Herophilus; and, an affair with Caenis, who, as a reward, was turned into an invulnerable man Caeneus and became king of the Lapiths.

Several of the offspring of these loves achieved fame: Pegasus, who carried Bellerophon to victory after victory, Neleus became father of Nestor, Pelias became a "heavy" in the Jason story, Nauplius learned how to navigate by the stars, Antaeus lost a wrestling match to Heracles, Polyphemus lost a girl to Acis and an eye to Odysseus, and Eumolpus, known for his musical and prophetic skills, founded the Eleusinian Mysteries.

Apollo: despite many attributes which would make him appear as an ideal lover, he encountered many problems. Except as noted, he had his own form in these stories.

Love	Offspring
1. Daphne, his first love	1. None
2. Rhoio (Rhoeo)	2. Anius
3. Creusa	3. Ion
4. Psamathe	4. Linus
5. Dryope: (as turtle, then snake, then self)	5. Amphissus
6. Chione: (as an old woman)	6. Philammon
7. Aria	7. Miletus
8. Cyrene	8. Aristaeus
9. Phthia	9. Dorus, Laodocus, Polypoetes
10. Coronis	10. Asclepius

Comments: Two stories in which Apollo's love was thwarted: Marpessa, who preferred the mortal Idas, and Cassandra, who changed her mind and was punished by having none believe her, even though Apollo, in anticipation, had given her the power to speak true prophecies (see *Agamemnon* by Aeschylus for her tragic end).

According to Ovid, Deione was mother of Miletus.

The Apollo-Coronis affair, like the Zeus-Semele story, resulted in the double birth of the offspring.

Two well-known homosexual love-stories involving Apollo were those of Cyparissus, who was turned into a cypress tree, and Hyacinth, who became a flower. In both cases, the young men were killed accidentally, were associated with Peloponnessus (Messenia and Sparta) , and were probably early local gods who had to be reconciled with the advent of Apollo.

Some of the offspring of these unions became quite famous: for example, Ion became the ancestor of the Ionians, Miletus founded a city, named for him, which produced some great figures, Aristaeus was the greatest bee-keeper of mythology, and Asclepius the greatest physician.

Ares: while enjoying the charms of Aphrodite, they were entrapped by Hephaestus, who called the other Olympians to see his "catch"; by Pyrene, Ares had Cycnus and by Cyrene, Diomedes (of Thrace) , both sons killed by Heracles; by Agraulos, Alcippe; by Astyoche, Ascalaphus and Ialmenus; by Demonice, Evenus, Molus, Pylus, and Thestius; by Althaea, Meleager (in some versions) . Aphrodite bore him Anteros, Harmonia, and (in some versions) Eros (Cupid) . As the Roman Mars, he became the father of Romulus and Remus by Rhea Silvia.

Aphrodite: Ares (see above) ; her two best-known mortal loves were with Adonis (see Ovid *Metamorphoses* 10) and Anchises, by whom she bore Aeneas. She was sometimes called the wife of Hephaestus (cf. Beauty and the Beast), but had affairs with Poseidon (see above) and Hermes, to whom she bore Hermaphroditus. Some accounts called Ares her husband and credited them with two other children, Phobos (Fear) and Deimos (Terror) .

Demeter: Zeus, and Poseidon (see above) ; by Iasion she bore Plutos (Wealth) .

Dionysus: by Ariadne, whom he married, he had many children; by Althea, Deianira (in some versions) .

Eos: by her husband, Tithonus, she bore Memnon and perhaps Phaëthon. An affair with Ares incurred the anger of Aphrodite, who caused Eos to fall in love with many mortals, among whom were Orion and Cephalus.

Helios: by Perse (or Perseis), he had Aeëtes, Circe, and Pasi-phaë; by Rhode, he had seven sons; by Clymene, or Eos, Phaë-thon. Clytie was changed into a heliotrope, and Leucothoë was buried alive by her father after an affair with Helios. By Neaera, he had Lampetia and Phaethusa.

Hephaestus: sometimes pictured as the unhappy husband of Aphrodite, although an old tradition paired him with Athena, who bore him Erichthonius. By Anticlea, he had Periphetes, who was killed by Theseus.

Hermes: Chione bore him Autolycus, the master-thief; Herse, Cephalus; Aphrodite, Hermaphroditus; Polymele, Eudorus; Phaethusa, or Clymene, Myrtilus, the fine chariot-driver.

Pan: involved in two well-known stories: Syrinx, who piped away, and Echo, who pined away.

Selene: had affairs with Zeus, Helios, and Pan. A famous story pairs her with Endymion, who produced 50 daughters and then fell eternally asleep.

Finally, two later tales of fun and frolic: Cupid and Psyche, and Pomona and Vertumnus; in both are elements of enterprise and surprise, with rather successful conclusions.

The point must again be made that this is not an all-inclusive list, yet enough to indicate that love stories in which the gods took part were very popular and, presumably, very *ex post facto*. The apparent lax morality of the gods brought amusement to the common men, subject-matter to the poets, and scorn to the philosophers, such as Plato. Christianity, agreeing with Plato's outlook, could ill afford to entrust literature dealing with these stories to its adherents. Eventually, however, a reconciliation did take place, though its time was long and its form various.

B. Quarrels and Battles of the Gods (or, "We're just one big happy family up here on Olympus")

The internal squabbles among the gods and goddesses kept their lives from becoming too dull or boring. Aside from the fact that too much togetherness proves the old saying that fa-miliarity breeds contempt, there were occasions and reasons for deities to lose patience with each other and, at times, even approach blows. Still, it was a rare day on Olympus which didn't end with a sumptuous banquet and hurt feelings soothed with nectar and ambrosia.

Two deities who seemed most to resent Zeus' power and, therefore, were the quickest to act or react unfavorably to him were Hera and Poseidon. Undoubtedly, the great power which each had enjoyed before the arrival of Zeus made her/him accept Zeus' supremacy with great reluctance and little enthusiasm. Hera and Zeus, in fact, seem to have spent most of their time arguing, although in all cases Zeus eventually won:

1. Hera, Zeus, and Troy: an ardent hater of Troy and all Trojans, Hera frequently upbraided Zeus for not doing more, and more quickly, to overthrow Troy. In *Iliad* 14, for example, she lures him away from the scene so that Poseidon can sneak down to aid the Greeks.

2. Tiresias settled one argument between Zeus and Hera by agreeing with Zeus that women find more pleasure than men in the sex act. Hera, enraged, blinded Tiresias, but Zeus gave him the power of prophecy.

3. Hera organized one revolt against Zeus and was subsequently punished by being suspended from heaven with gold bracelets on her wrists and anvils on her feet. After securing a promise of no more such revolts, Zeus restored her to Olympus.

4. Hera, Poseidon and Athena conspired against Zeus and bound him in bed. In this instance, Thetis and Briareus released Zeus and helped him gain control again.

5. Hera was a constant foe of Zeus' lovers and the children of these affairs. She managed to have Semele killed, for example, and she hounded Heracles throughout his life.

6. After Zeus produced Athena unaided, Hera produced Hephaestus unaided: thus, equality of the sexes was proved at an early date. Hephaestus was made lame by having been thrown down from Olympus either by Zeus (because Hephaestus tried to rescue his mother during the revolt) or by Hera (who didn't like his lack of beauty and grace).

7. Just as Greek Hera constantly "needled" Zeus throughout the *Iliad,* so Roman Juno "needled" Jupiter throughout the *Aeneid.* In both cases the god's will and rule prevailed after heated exchanges of words and threats.

8. For the part Poseidon and Apollo played in the revolt, Zeus consigned them to help build the city walls of Troy. After King Laomedon reneged on his promise of pay, Poseidon sent a sea-monster to ravage the country until such time as Laomedon sacrificed his daughter Hesione to the monster; in the nick of time, Heracles arrived, killed the beast, and rescued Hesione. Poseidon's relentless hatred of Troy, however, continued throughout the Trojan War.

9. Poseidon engaged in a number of contests with other Olympians for the patronage of cities: he lost to Athena for Athens, tied with her for Troezen, lost to Hera for Argos and to Apollo for Delphi, and tied with Helios for Corinth.

10. Poseidon brought Ares to trial on a charge of murder: Ares had allegedly killed a son of Poseidon, Hallirrhothios, for violating his daughter, Alcippe. Ares was acquitted.

11. Apollo became angry after Zeus killed his son Asclepius for reviving Hippolytus; in retaliation, he killed the Cyclops who had made the thunderbolt used by Zeus. Zeus, in turn, banished Apollo from Olympus, and, for some time, Apollo served as a shepherd for the flocks of King Admetus of Thessaly.

12. A feminine battle of wits was pictured by Virgil, as he described the concern of Venus and Juno over Aeneas: Venus wants her son to accomplish his task of refounding the Trojan line in Italy, while Juno hopes to prevent it.

13. The gods battled away against each other during the Trojan War: Aphrodite and Apollo fought with Trojans, Athena, Poseidon and Hera with Greeks, Ares now with one side, now with the other. When wounded, they were miraculously healed; the only undignified god in the action was Ares. (*Iliad* 20 and 21)

14. One humorous episode occurred when Hera, having seated herself in a new chair built for her by Hephaestus, discovered she couldn't get up; Hephaestus, angered by his fall, had fashioned the chair with invisible bonds. Only through the intervention of Dionysos did Hephaestus finally release his mother.

As the sun set beyond Mt. Olympus, however, there was music and laughter, after which all went home to bed; "Zeus, lord of lightning, . . . settled down for the night, with Hera of the golden throne beside him." (*Iliad* 1)

C. Some combats in which the gods participated may be conveniently listed here:

1. the Olympians vs. the Titans (except Prometheus)
2. the Olympians vs. the Giants; vs. Typhon; vs. the Aloads
3. Apollo vs. Python (snake or dragon) at Delphi; founding of the Pythian Games
4. Apollo and Artemis vs. Tityus; this would-be attacker of Leto was killed and staked out in the Lower World, where his body covered nine acres. Vultures ate of his liver (or heart) every day.
5. Apollo vs. Phorbas, the boxer, who profaned the temple at Delphi
6. Artemis vs. Orion: (many conflicting stories)
7. Diomedes attacked even gods in his rampaging onslaught in *Iliad* 5, winding up by wounding both Aphrodite and Ares.

Finally, it is to be noted that the world's first beauty contest, in which the participants were Aphrodite, Athena, and Hera, was caused by Eris the goddess of strife, and resulted in the Trojan War. Perhaps the golden apple was really a lemon!

CHAPTER 5

Gods, Mortals, and Death

As we have noted earlier, although there were some characteristics shared commonly by gods and men, there were others which kept them far apart. Occasionally, however, mortals might dare to breach the gulf between them and the gods by trying to make themselves equal to the gods, by challenging the gods, or by attempting super-human feats. The sin thus perpetrated by the mortals was *hubris,* excessive pride or arrogance, the most detested of all offences. Those guilty of *hubris* invariably were punished with *ate,* blindness or ruin, often administered by Nemesis, the goddess of Retribution, or by the Erinyes acting as agents of Zeus, or by other mortals serving as special agents of the gods. Certainly, the study of Greek tragedy shows the many forms *hubris* and *ate* can take. Even heroes were not immune from this sin, as the case of Bellerophon illustrates. Among mortals, Xerxes, the Great King of Persia, was a prime example of *hubris* and its punishment, as Herodotus so well pointed out.

In spite of the fact that anyone might be guilty of *hubris,* there was at least one strong deterrent, aside from the thought of punishment. The deterrent was to accept one's limitations, and, within those limitations to live in accordance with the two most basic Greek doctrines, "Know Thyself" and "Nothing in Excess." By observance to these basic concepts, mortals could acquire *arete,* moral excellence, and *sophrosune,* reasonableness.

I. Sins and punishments of mortals

A. Pretending to be Zeus or Zeus and Hera

Sinner	Sin	Punishment
1. Salmoneus	1. Claimed self better than Zeus	1. Hit by Zeus' bolt and put into Lower World
2. Ceyx and Alcyone	2. Happier than Zeus and Hera	2. Turned into sea-birds
3. Polytechnos and Aedon	3. Happier than Zeus and Hera	3. They and son turned into birds at Hera's instigation
4. Haemus and Rhodope	4. Happier than Zeus and Hera	4. Turned into adjacent mountains

B. Presumption, or going beyond god-given powers

Sinner	Sin	Punishment
1. Asclepius	1. Restored Hippolytus to life	1. Killed by Zeus' thunder-bolt
2. Daedalus	2. Made wings for self and son and flew	2. Son Icarus killed: (Icarian Sea)
3. Ocyrrhoë	3. Prophecies too true	3. Changed into mare called Hippo
4. Phaëthon	4. Driving Sun-chariot	4. Killed by Zeus' thunder-bolt
5. Phineus	5. Prophecies too true	5. Blinded by Zeus and visited by Harpies
6. Tantalus	6. Gave nectar and ambrosia to mortals	6. Unable to drink water in which he stood or eat fruit from overhanging trees (water and fruit receded)
7. Prometheus	7. Gave fire to man	7. Chained to Caucasus; eagle ate his liver each day
8. Patroclus	8. Became too bold in battle	8. Killed by Hector and Apollo

C. Offending, neglecting, or denying a god or his/her power

Sinner	Sin	Punishment
1. Pentheus	1. Tried to keep worship of Dionysus out of Thebes	1. Torn apart by worshippers of Dionysus, including his mother (Bacchae of Euripides)

Sinner	Sin	Punishment
2. Lydian Pirates	2. Captured Dionysus and hoped to sell him as slave	2. Turned into dolphins by Dionysus
3. Lycurgus	3. Opposed worship of Dionysus	3. Driven mad by Dionysus, he killed his son
4. Daughters of Minyas	4. Refused to worship Dionysus	4. Turned into bats by Dionysus
5. 3 daughters of Proteus	5. Refused to worship Dionysus	5. Maddened by Dionysus, but cured by Melampus
6. Lycians	6. Refused water to Leto	6. Turned into frogs by Leto
7. Erysichthon	7. Refused to spare sacred tree	7. Given insatiable appetite by Demeter, he ate himself
8. Pirithous	8. Neglected offerings to Ares	8. Ares caused a riot at wedding festivities
9. Tantalus	9. Tested omnisience of gods by serving them his son at banquet	9. Placed in water and under fruit trees, he can't eat or drink
10. Sisyphus	10. Tried to cheat Hades and death	10. Put into Tartarus where he continues to push the rock which always rolls down again
11. Momus	11. Criticized the gods too freely	11. Driven from Olympus
12. Lycaon	12. Taunted Zeus	12. Turned into wolf by Zeus
13. 5 naiads	13. Failed to sacrifice to Artemis	13. Became islands, called the Echidnes
14. Cassandra	14. Reneged on promise to Apollo	14. No one would believe her true prophecies
15. Hippolytus	15. Denied Aphrodite's power	15. Killed after being falsely accused by Phaedra
16. Rhoecus	16. Injured messenger-bee of dryad lover	16. Blinded by the dryad
17. Phlegyas	17. Violated Delphic shrine	17. Killed by Apollo and put in Tartarus under rock which always threatens to fall

Other examples could be cited, but the above suffice to show that the gods resent mortals' neglect or denial. Dionysus, Aphrodite, and Apollo frequently had to crush non-believers in or belittlers of their power (see Ovid's *Metamorphoses* especially for sins against Venus).

D. Challenging a god

Sinner	Deity and challenge	Punishment
1. Arachne	1. Athena: contest in spinning and weaving	1. Turned into spider
2. 9 daughters of King Pierus in Thessaly (Pierides)	2. Muses: singing	2. Turned into magpies
3. Thamyris	3. Muses: singing	3. Blinded
4. Sirens	4. Muses: singing	4. Had feathers plucked out and made into crowns for the Muses
5. Misenus	5. Triton: horn-playing	5. Drowned
6. Marsyas	6. Apollo: flute-playing	6. Flayed alive; mourners' tears formed river
7. Midas	7. Insisted that Pan's playing was superior to Apollo's	7. Given ears of an ass
8. Orion	8. Artemis: game of darts	8. Killed by giant scorpion
9. Erechtheus	9. Delayed wedding of daughter Orithyia to Boreas	9. Boreas carried off Orithyia to Thrace and married her

E. Sins against goddesses

Sinner	Sin	Punishment
1. Actaeon	1. Saw Artemis bathing	1. Turned into stag and killed by own hounds
2. Tiresias	2. Saw Athena bathing	2. Blinded
3. Minthe	3. Wooed Hades	3. Turned into mint by Persephone
4. Ixion	4. Tried to win love of Hera	4. Chained to ever-rolling wheel in Tartarus
5. Tityus	5. Violence against Leto	5. Killed by Apollo and Artemis and staked out over 9 acres in the Lower World
6. Orion	6. Violence against Artemis (or Leto)	6. Killed by arrows of Artemis

F. Boasting

Sinner	Boast	Punishment
1. Niobe	1. Her number of children	1. Children killed by Artemis and Apollo; she was turned into ever-weeping rock
2. Lethaea	2. Beauty	2. She and husband turned into stone by the gods
3. Medusa	3. Beautiful hair	3. Given snaky locks by Athena
4. Laodamia	4. Had borne a son to Zeus	4. Killed by Artemis
5. Myrrha's Mother	5. That Myrrha was more beautiful than Aphrodite	5. Given unnatural love for her father
6. Cassiopeia	6. She and her daughter Andromeda more lovely than Nereids	6. Poseidon sent sea-monster to ravage land

Despite the obvious lessons to be learned from the past, numerous historical figures considered themselves gods or close associates of gods. Alexander the Great requested that he be thought of as a god, and later he (or his propagandists) claimed him to be the son of Zeus-Ammon. In his own mind, however, he was a reincarnation of Heracles or Dionysos, since he was freeing peoples everywhere of fear—except, of course, the fear of Alexander the Great.

The Romans began the practice of deification with Romulus, who was considered the god Quirinus after his disappearance in a thunderstorm. Julius Caesar associated himself with Jupiter, in addition to his frequent references he was descended from Venus, through Aeneas and Julus. (It was only blood that poured out on March 15, 44 B. C.) Caesar was considered a god after July, 44 B. C., when his soul was seen rising to heaven by thousands of Romans. Mark Antony regarded himself as Dionysos, but he was really a drunken sot; further, he and Cleopatra named their twins Alexander Helios and Cleopatra Selene, a touching but pointless gesture. Sextus Pompey gave himself the cognomen Neptunius because of his success in naval warfare; after his defeat at sea, he was rather embarrassed. Augustus, emperor from 27 B. C. to 14 A. D., allied himself closely to Apollo, and thus signified Rome as the new center of "light" and civilization; he was also honored with deification after death. Nero's boasting of his creative talent must have offended some god, for we hear of an occasional earthquake or storm near the scene of his concerts. An ultimate of sorts was achieved, however, when Domitian (81-96 A.D.) proclaimed that he was to be addressed with the title *Dominus et Deus* (Lord and God) ; he, too, was mortal, as the conspiracy led by his wife proved. Finally, we may note one instance in which it did not pay to advertise: the emperor Commodus (180-192 A. D.) announced that he was Hercules incarnate and would demonstrate his amazing virtuosity in the Amphitheater on January 1, 193; henceforth his name was to be Hercules Romanus, and a bust of him with accoutrements of Heracles was duly readied. Alas, before January 1, 193, he was strangled by an athlete named Narcissus, who had been hired for the task by the emperor's advisors. *Sic transit gloria mundi.*

II. Dying Gods and Mystery Rites

This sub-title is at one and the same time miraculous and mysterious, yet it mentions two concepts which have appeared in many civilizations, including our own. The idea of a dying-and-rising god goes back to the Ancient Near East, where Osiris in Egypt and Tammuz in Babylonia fulfilled the role. Mystery rites, in which certain initiatory rituals were needed for admission, probably go back to religious feelings ante-dating even the dying-and-rising god idea. Both concepts may be properly designated as religious, if religion is broadly defined as an effort to make sense of a mysterious world and to establish good relations with the mysterious powers that control the world. It appears, then, that mystery rites and dying gods evolved out of the basic duality of man to feel with his emotions and to reason with his mind.

In wider perspective, religion itself—while it may to some extent satisfy man's curiosity and soothe his worries about misfortune, illness and death—may be a balance, *dikê* (as Sophocles called it) , between rational and irrational, mystery and revelation, darkness and light, Olympian gods and chthonian powers, even East and West. Perhaps this is the inherent idea in the "Sacred Marriage" mentioned earlier. Hera, as a pre-Greek earth-mother goddess was wedded to Zeus, the Greek sky-father god. And, although sophisticated people in Greek cities fancied Zeus as the stronger member of the pair, Hera was the stronger in the country-side, where all things came from the earth and returned to the earth. Further, no amount of intellectualizing or verbalizing could fully explain the powers responsible for birth, growth, reproduction, and death. The ground giveth, the ground storeth, and the ground keepeth; even man, with all his capacities, still walked with feet firmly anchored to the ground, and, after death, was deposited finally in the ground. Yet, if corn or grain could die in the fields, be kept in underground siloes, then brought out, replanted, and begin a renewed life, could not the same thing be expected for man? Corn was buried but was not dead; perhaps man's burial was not the end. All nature, in fact, underwent a similar cycle of birth, death and rebirth, with the exception of certain trees and vines which remained ever vigorous and ever green. Thus, when the rest of nature apparently died, some trees and vines reminded mankind that not all had died, that there was hope, that death had not conquered life absolutely, that there was a balance between life and death. Gods might die, but they rose again; mortals, too, might rise after death, but their chances were better if they had been initiated into the mystery rites and had obtained some glimpse or understanding of the mysteries of this world.

Among the more prominent dying-and-rising gods were the following, many of whose careers showed a miraculous birth, a brief career, a violent death, and resurrection:

1. Adonis: perhaps akin Tammuz, his name seems derived from the Phoenician *adon,* meaning lord. Byblus was his possible origin, and from there his worship went to Cyprus and thence to Greece. As the offspring of the illicit affair between king Cinyras of Cyprus and his daughter Myrrha, Adonis was born from the trunk of the tree into which his mother had been changed (thus the myth told). A handsome young man, loved by Aphrodite, he one day wounded a boar, which turned on him and killed him. Aphrodite, hurrying to his cries of pain, scratched her ankle on the thorn of a rose bush, and the roses promptly turned from white to red. Adonis died, but his blood was transformed into the anemone, the "wind-flower," which enjoys a brief life, then dies.

A variant says that Aphrodite entrusted the infant Adonis to Persephone with instructions not to open the chest in which Adonis lay. Persephone did open the chest, however, saw Adonis and refused to give him back to Aphrodite at the appointed time. In the ensuing argument, Zeus decreed Adonis would spend one-third of the year with Persephone, one-third with Aphrodite, and have one-third to himself, (or half the year with Persephone and half with Aphrodite).

The worship of Adonis, connected with Aphrodite, came to Athens in the 5th century B. C., and a yearly festival representing his death and resurrection, the Adonia, was held in mid-summer.

2. Attis (or Atys) : his origin was Phrygia, and his birth (in one version) came as the result of a river-nymph Nana eating an almond. As a handsome young man, he became the consort of the great goddess Cybele, who hoped to keep him exclusively hers. Though he had sworn an oath of fidelity to Cybele, Attis one day forgot the oath and made love to a tree nymph, Sagaritis. Cybele, enraged, cut down the tree, thereby killing Sagaritis, and drove Attis mad. In this state, Attis went to the top of a mountain, emasculated himself, and died at the base of a pine tree. His blood was changed into violets, which later were a part of the festival in his honor. (Another story says he was killed by a wild boar.) Attis seldom appears in Greek myth or religion, but in Rome, his orgiastic festival was given official sanction by the emperor Claudius (41-54 A.D.). His festival occurred March 22-27, the time considered to be the Spring equinox, and was notorious for its excesses. Its central theme was the death and resurrection of Attis. (see Catullus, Poem 63)

3. Demeter, Persephone, Hades: the best-known Greek story of a dying-and-returning deity; (notice here that the central figure is female, and that many elements of the earlier stories are absent). Persephone, carried away to the Lower World by Hades, could not return to the Upper World, since she had eaten pomegranate seeds. The sorrowing mother, Demeter, forgot this world and its concerns as she searched for her daughter. Having found her, she could not persuade Hades to give up his new queen;

Zeus, however, ruled that Persephone should spend part of the year with her mother and part with her husband. Demeter, pleased with the decision, renewed her interest in this world and caused the erstwhile dead crops to spring back to life. She expressed her particular thanks to the city of Eleusis by establishing there her mystery rites. Eumolpus, famous for his musical skill, became the first chief priest of the Eleusinian Mysteries, and his descendants carried on the tradition of serving as priests of Demeter. The mysteries themselves remained the most attractive of all such rites in antiquity, even to such noble Romans as Cicero and Hadrian. Modern scholars have offered convincing evidence that the rite centered around the exhibiting of corn; certainly, all initiates kept its secrets guarded and believed that they would enjoy a happier life after death because of their initiation into the mysteries.

4. Dionysos: had a miraculous double birth as the son of Zeus and Semele. As in most of the above stories, we know nothing about the young years of Dionysos, though his origin may have been Thrace (or Phrygia). As we have seen, his advent into Greece occasioned fierce opposition; in time, however, his adjustment to the Greek view became so complete that he shared the temple at Delphi with Apollo, the most Greek of the Greek gods. According to a common account, Dionysos was killed by Titans, who tore him apart, roasted the pieces, and began to eat. Zeus managed to save some of the pieces, and he gave them to Apollo to bury at Delphi. There, it was believed, Dionysos arose each year from the dead and reigned during the three winter months, while Apollo was away.

The essential parts of the worship of Dionysos consisted of *ecstasy* and *enthusiasm,* that is, the actual "standing outside of oneself" (*ecstasy*) and the god's temporary presence within one (*enthusiasm*). Euripides in the *Bacchae* presents an unforgettable picture of the ritual in his honor, in which women were the participants who, as a climax, ate the flesh and drank the blood of an animal, believing they were actually partaking of the god.

Many stories attested the travels of Dionysos and his attempts to better the condition of man by teaching him the arts of viniculture and wine-making. His worship came to Rome at an early date, for we have a Roman inscription of 186 B. C. banning the Bacchanalia. (The name Bacchus may have come from Lydia, or it may have originated in the name (or cry) Iacchus, a deity closely associated with the Eleusinian Mysteries.) The attempt to suppress this orgiastic rite proved as unsuccessful in Italy as it had earlier in Greece. It always had special appeal to women, and it was quite popular in Rome during the 1st century A. D.

5. Heracles: although not known as well as the above in rituals suggesting life after death, he was nevertheless most important as an example—the supreme example, in fact—of a mortal who by his courageous deeds earned immortal life. His career followed the familiar pattern of miraculous birth, overcoming many obstacles, violent death, and resurrection. As is noted elsewhere, three of his 12 Labors and at least one other story show him overcoming death itself. Obviously, his credentials warranted admission to Olympus or heaven.

6. Others: there were many local gods in antiquity who served much the same function as those just named. The fact that their stories were localized should not at all detract from their importance; after all, many medieval Christians were as staunchly faithful to local saints as to God.

Anyone wishing to pursue the careers or rites of the dying-and-saving gods would do well to begin his investigation with Sir James Frazer's *The Golden Bough*. Although modern scholars disagree with parts of Frazer's work, it should be read, both for its style and content.

III. Myths of the Lower World

As evidence mounts, and archaeologists and philologists continue their research, it becomes clear that man has always been concerned with two worlds, this in which he found himself and that in which he might find himself after this life. Our earliest predecessors, the Sumerians, had stories about the Lower World, and some of their ideas about that region of after-life were transmitted from the third millenium B. C. onward to

Babylonian and other literature. The fascinating tale of how the Sumerian account has been pieced together may be found in Samuel Noah Kramer's *Sumerian Mythology*.

In the Sumerian story, Inanna, queen of heaven and goddess of light, love and life, intends to visit the Lower World. The queen of that "land of no return" is Ereshkigal, goddess of darkness, gloom and death, and Inanna's older sister. As Inanna draws near Ereshkigal's temple, the chief gatekeeper demands an explanation, is apparently satisfied with Inanna's false story, and leads her through the 7 gates of the Lower World. At each gate part of Inanna's clothes and jewels are taken off (over her protests), and she appears naked before Ereshkigal and the 7 judges of the Lower World. The latter fix their "look of death" upon her, and as a corpse she is hung from a stake. After three days and three nights had been spent in this position, help arrived in the persons of two sexless creatures who sprinkled their "food of life" and "water of life" 60 times upon Inanna's corpse. The revival, planned by Enki, the god of water and wisdom, is successful, and Inanna begins her ascent, accompanied by shades of the dead and by various creatures which inhabit the Lower World. With this entourage she travels from city to city. At this point the poem breaks off.

Among later Greeks and Romans, bound by no dogma or revelation, numerous and often contradictory concepts of the after-life existed side by side. There must have been a certain convenience, therefore, since one could believe or not believe as he chose, and, if he did believe, he could accept the account which most suited his own ideas. The literary accounts preserved for us however, are not so numerous or divergent; while these do not agree on many details, a consistent picture does emerge of the land in which souls dwell, and a developing refinement of ideas is traceable.

A. Homer

1. *Iliad* 23: the ghost of Patroclus appears to sleeping Achilles. (Note emphasis upon resemblance of the ghost to the living Patroclus, and Patroclus' request for burial.)
2. *Odyssey* 4: the first extant reference to Elysium, and the suggestion that there dwell blessed souls who live a life of ease under a perpetually good climate.

3. *Odyssey* 10: Circe's instructions to Odysseus on how to get to the Land of the Dead and what to do after he arrives there. Four rivers are mentioned: Styx, Acheron, Pyriphlegethon, and Cocytus. (Notice the rituals which must be performed to evoke the shades of the dead.)

4. *Odyssey* 11: Odysseus with the shades of the dead: he speaks, in succession, to Elpenor, Tiresias, Agamemnon, Achilles and Ajax. He sees other shades at work or being punished: Minos, Orion, Tityos, Tantalus, Sisyphus. Heracles appears, addresses Odysseus, and leaves. Odysseus becomes alarmed and quickly sails back to Circe's island. (Note the characteristics of the shades: they are like smoke, shadows or dreams; they have no bones, flesh or strength; they usually utter a shrill cry, but, after drinking blood, they can speak. They can be seen and heard, yet they are not substantial enough to be grasped (cf. *Iliad* 23). They have memories and emotions, and may be thought of as dim counterparts of the living.) In this passage occurs the well-known sentiment of Achilles: "I'd rather be hired out (as a slave) than serve as the door-keeper of the dead."

B. **Hesiod,** *Works and Days* 167 ff.: some who had lived in the Age of Heroes were transported by Zeus to an abode apart from men, at the ends of the earth. There, by the shores of Ocean, these men live without sorrow, fed by grain and fruit (provided three times a year by earth), far removed from the deathless gods, ruled over by Kronos, and with glory and honor.

C. **Plato,** *Republic* 10: the Vision of Er, the soldier who had apparently died but returned to life in order to tell men about life after death and life after life. Drawing upon Homer, Pythagoras and the cult of Orphism, Plato pictured a much more complex and spiritualized existence. Souls of the good and bad go to different areas, either heaven or hell; after 1,000 years, souls draw lots to determine what life they will lead next. Their choices made and ratified, they drink of the river Lethe (first mention in literature of this river) and are born again amid night, thunder, and earthquake. (Notice that Plato uses the whole section to point up the idea that justice has rewards and punishments in life and after death.)

D. Virgil, *Aeneid* 6: Aeneas, guided by Sibyl, must go to the Lower World to talk with the shade of his father Anchises. Three tasks must be done before he can leave for the Lower World: burial of a dead companion, picking up the golden bough, and sacrificing black cows. Virgil's picture is detailed and graphic: the personified causes of death; the hybrid monsters encountered; meeting Charon ferrying the souls of the dead and passage over the Acheron river; getting by Cerberus; the main areas of the Lower World, each with its own judge:

(1.) Mourning Fields, where Minos rules, in which dwell suicides, those falsely accused, infants, unwed girls, and heroes;

(2.) Tartarus, where Rhadamanthus rules, in which sinners against gods, traitors, and evil-doers undergo everlasting punishment; the whole area, pictured as the opposite of the Golden Age, is circled by the River of Fire (Phlegethon) and three strong walls, and is guarded by the Furies;

(3.) The Elysian Fields, where Aeacus apparently rules, in which ordinary good men and heroes lead a pleasant and contented existence. Nearby is the Lethe River, from which entering and departing souls must drink. Souls must be cleansed of all sins and, after living there 100 years, may have new lives. Anchises reveals the future of Rome to Aeneas, who leaves before midnight.

Later authors, such as Dante, Tasso, Spencer, and Milton, relied rather heavily on the ancient authors for their glimpses of the Lower World (or Otherworld), but added from their own imaginations and backgrounds.

From these condensed mythological stories let us turn to other stories of the Lower World. The majority of these, it may be noticed, have also the theme of descent and return but emphasize the relationship between love and death:

1. Alcestis and Admetus: love of wife rescues husband, and Heracles rescues wife; (see Euripides, *Alcestis*).

2. Orpheus and Eurydice: love and the power of music almost triumph over death.

3. Odysseus: to talk with Tiresias; (his conversation with the shade of his mother is beautifully drawn by Homer).

4. Aeneas: to talk with the shade of Anchises, his father; (en route he sees and talks to the shade of Dido).

5. Heracles: to carry up Cerberus, as one of his 12 Labors; (possible rescue of Alcestis and freeing of Theseus).

6. Theseus and Pirithous: to carry off Persephone as a bride for Pirithous.

7. Psyche: to borrow some of the beauty secrets of Persephone; (much later, beauty aids for ladies were thought to come from the Devil).

8. Persephone herself: to rule part-time as queen and wife of Hades.

9. Sisyphus: who entered the Lower World dead, but, by a ruse, returned to life; Ares forced his return, however, and, as punishment for this attempted escape, Sisyphus had to roll the huge rock up the hill time after time *ad infinitum*.

10. Protesilaus: was allowed a short return to be with his wife, after which they descended together.

Sinners frequently depicted as occupying Tartarus, the place of torment for the wicked, include:

1. Titans, Giants, Typhon, all enemies of the gods.

2. Tityus, whose liver was plucked out each day by vultures.

3. Tantalus, who could reach neither food nor water.

4. Ixion, chained to an ever-turning wheel.

5. Phlegyas, above whose head hung a stone about to fall.

6. Pirithous, forever fastened to a rock, or to a chair of forgetfulness.

7. 49 of the 50 daughters of Danaus, forever carrying water in sieves, as punishment for killing their husbands on their wedding night. (Their husbands were the 50 sons of Aegyptus; only Hyperm(n)estra disobeyed her father's order and helped her husband Lynceus escape; see Aeschylus, *Suppliants*.)

Features and creatures frequently mentioned in connection with the Lower World:

1. The rivers: Pyriphlegethon (or Phlegethon), the River of Fire; Acheron, the River of Woe; Cocytus, the River of Wailing; Lethe, the River of Forgetfulness; Styx, the Hated River (and river by which the gods swore oaths).

2. The areas: Mourning Fields, Tartarus, Elysian Fields.
3. The guardians: Charon, Cerberus, Erinyes (Furies), Hecate.
4. The judges: Minos, Rhadamanthus, Aeacus; (Plato mentions Triptolemus as a judge).
5. Lamia: fond of destroying children and luring young men.
6. Empusae: vampires who could assume disguises and devoured their lovers.
7. Personified causes of death.
8. Sleep and Dreams.

Finally, we might recall the admonition of Sibyl to Aeneas: "Easy is the descent to the Lower World; but, to retrace your steps and to escape to the upper air—this is the task, this the toil."

CHAPTER 6

Myths of the Sea

Since the history of both the pre-Greek and the Greek peoples was so largely determined by the sea, it is not surprising that there were many myths having to do with the sea and travel over the sea. The countries bordering the Mediterranean, due to this important waterway, have developed a higher civilization—among others the Minoan civilization of Crete. Recently, the image of a Mycenaean dagger has been found in Stonehenge, England. (The Minoan-Mycenaean civilizations may be dated from c. 1600-1100 B. C.) In the early 5th century B. C., Themistocles convinced Athens that her strength must be placed in her navy, and, before long, Athens had won control of the sea and had fashioned an empire. In 146 B. C. Rome eliminated the last of her rivals, Carthage in the west and Corinth in the east, and she assumed complete domination of the Mediterranean region: the Mediterranean had become, as Rome called it, *Mare Nostrum* (Our Sea) .

In earlier times, however, the seas was the avenue for adventure and daring, the path for advancing, retreating, or homecoming. Historians could later tell of the colonization and commercial development made possible by the sea; to the early races, it was the capricious realm which, hopefully, man would some day subdue, just as he had subdued so much of nature (see Sophocles, *Antigone* 332 ff.) .

The lord of this realm was Poseidon, who had as his wife, the Nereid, Amphitrite. Poseidon could unleash terrible wrath, as Homer showed in the *Iliad* and the *Odyssey;* in the latter work, Odysseus was the object of the god's unending anger for having blinded Polyphemus, the cyclops-son of Poseidon. All of the cunning and wisdom of Odysseus had to be employed before he finally arrived, alone and in need, at Ithaca. Even then,

Poseidon had the last word by turning to stone the ship which had carried Odysseus home. On the other hand, Poseidon could be a friendly deity, as Virgil showed him in Book 1 of the *Aeneid*. After the great storm had scattered the fleet of Aeneas, Poseidon (Neptune) calmed the waters, chased away the winds, and helped men and ships to safety. Like the sea itself, Poseidon could be destructive or beneficial; yet, he was not the only deity of the deep to whom mortals could turn for assistance. Other gods and goddesses certainly could not equal the authority of Poseidon, but they could and did become important figures in the world of myth.

I. The "Old Men of the Sea," and the "White Goddess"

The Greek idea of the *Halioi Gerontes,* "the old men of the sea," equipped with special powers of wisdom and fore-knowledge, may have derived from the Sumerian god of wisdom, Enki, who was, as well, the god of the sea.

A. Proteus: herded seals and other sea flocks; had knowledge of the future which he would reveal only to those who could out-wrestle him, and, since he could change shapes at will, beating him was not easy. Heracles, Menelaus, and Aristaeus were three who successfully obtained information from him. The favorite haunt of Proteus was the Carpathian Sea.

B. Nereus: famous for his 50 daughters, (by Doris), called Nereids; he too had prophetic powers and could change shapes. Pictured with a long, flowing beard, azure hair, and dwelling chiefly in the Aegean Sea, he was sometimes referred to as the most ancient of all gods. Heracles and Paris received information from him.

C. Glaucus: originally a fisherman, he tasted a certain grass or herb which caused him to want to live in the sea. Having jumped in, he became a deity, and an attendant of Poseidon. His subsequent love affair, involving Scylla and Circe, was well-known; he did have prophetic powers, and he was regarded as the father of the Sibyl of Cumae.

D. Phorcys: married his sister Ceto and by her, became the father of the Gorgons, the Graiae, the Sirens, and Scylla. He was frequently considered the leader of the Tritons, the male attendants of Poseidon.

E. Thaumas: married the Oceanid Electra, and became by her the father of the Harpies and Iris, the messenger of the gods.

F. "White Goddess," Leukothea: many sites had myths similar to the story of Leucothea, and, in all such myths, the elements of pursuit and flight, a plunge into the sea, and transformation into a deity are to be seen. Leucothea was originally a mortal woman Ino, who, to escape the madness of her husband Athamas, jumped into the sea with her son Melicertes; both were turned into sea deities —Ino into Leucothea, Melicertes into Palaemon. In some versions of the story, Heracles was a participant, (see, for example, Ovid's *Fasti* 6.473-562; compare with this account, Ovid's *Metamorphoses* 4.416-562). The Roman authors of the Augustan Age often allude to Leucothea and/or Palaemon as deities who will protect sailors and who may be found anywhere in the sea. In 1956, however, excavations on the Isthmus of Corinth revealed a temple to Palaemon, which was probably built some time in the reign of Augustus (27 B. C.-14 A. D.). An extant inscription says the temple was built by Publius Licinius Priscus Iuventianus; coins of the same period illustrate the temple together with Palaemon and a dolphin, a pine-tree, a priest, and a sacrificial bull. These latter accoutrements were necessary for the rites, which took place at night and resembled those to a chthonic deity.

From the time of Augustus, Palaemon was closely associated with Corinth, as numerous literary references attest (see, for example, Pausanias 2.1-6). Among the Romans, Palaemon became identified with Portunus, the god of harbors.

II. A number of sea-myths dealt with the subject of love. Among these, the following are perhaps the better known:

1. Arethusa: escaped the advances of Achelous by going underground and underseas and emerging on the island of Sicily, near Syracuse; there she became a patroness goddess, closely associated with Artemis. Coins represented them with companion dolphins.

2. Aesacus: this son of Priam hoped to win the love of the sea-nymph Hesperia (or Asterope); she fled, but was bit-

ten by a snake and died. He, (or both), was turned into a sea-bird.

3. Ceyx and Alcyone: according to Ovid, *Metamorphoses* 11.587 ff., Ceyx was drowned en route to an oracle; Alcyone, informed by Morpheus, sought the body of Ceyx, found it, and jumped into the sea to be with him. Both were changed into birds. (cf. "halcyon days")

4. Polyphemus, Galataea and Acis: Polyphemus had a "crush," and Acis was crushed.

III. Even in antiquity, dolphins were regarded as loveable, helpful creatures. Their habit of pushing up their young suggested the "saving" characteristic of the dolphins. Modern science has discovered that dolphins are easily trained and are possessed of high intelligence; soon, perhaps the "talking" of the dolphins will be decoded, and another facet of these quite remarkable creatures will be known. The ancients considered dolphins a sort of good-luck charm while traveling and told stories about them, such as the following:

1. Melicertes: carried to the Isthmus of Corinth, he became a god.

2. Amphitrite: her whereabouts was revealed to Poseidon by a dolphin (in one version).

3. Arion: perhaps a real poet, he was snatched from death by dolphins who conducted him to safety; later, he gained his revenge on the pirates who had tried to kill him.

4. Hesiod: a story concerning his death said that he was thrown into the sea after death, but that dolphins brought his body back to land for proper burial.

5. Enalos and Phineis: lovers saved by dolphins.

6. Telemachus: a story says that, as a boy, he fell into the sea but was brought safely to shore by a dolphin.

(We have no record, as far as I know, of a dolphin jumping through a hoop or playing basket-ball in antiquity.)

IV. Two "Salty Dogs": either of the two might have been an ancient "Popeye," for both were popular figures renowned for their voyages and escapades.

A. Jason, captain of the *Argo*, (often considered the world's first sea-going vessel): Jason's patron goddess, Hera.

1. The background of Jason: Aeson and Pelias and the oracle, "Beware of a man wearing one sandal."

2. Reason for the trip, (a quest myth) : to obtain the Golden Fleece.
   (a) Phrirxus, Helle, Nephele, and Athamas: rescue in the nick of time.
   (b) How the Hellespont received its name.
3. The Argonauts, 50 of the best men and heroes.
4. Building of the *Argo,* equipped with a talking prow.
5. The journey to Colchis, the land of King Aeëtes.
   (a) The stop at Lemnos to visit the Lemnian women: Hypsipyle.
   (b) Death of King Cyzicus, a regretful accident.
   (c) Loss of Hylas and Heracles.
   (d) Amycus, victim of the shortest knock-out in history, administered by Polydeuces.
   (e) King Phineus: Harpies routed by Boreads, (Zetes and Calais) .
   (f) Through the Symplegades and on to Colchis.
6. Seizure of the Golden Fleece: Aeëtes' requirements, and aid from Medea.
   (a) Departure of the Argonauts at night, accompanied by Medea and her brother Absyrtus (or Apsyrtus) .
   (b) Pursuit of Aeëtes, death of Absyrtus, and safety for Jason.
7. The journey home to Thessaly: the *Argo* sails in almost every navigable sea, ocean, river and stream.
   (a) The Clashing (or Wandering) Rocks.
   (b) Orpheus surpasses the Sirens.
   (c) Passage between Scylla and Charybdis.
   (d) Following the *Argo's* advice, purification for death of Absyrtus on the island of Circe.
   (e) Official marriage of Jason and Medea.
   (f) The Talos affair, in which Medea again prevails.
8. Home at last, then on to Corinth.
   (a) Death of Pelias, drained of life.
   (b) Departure of Jason and Medea from Thessaly.
   (c) Golden Fleece deposited in temple of Zeus in Orchomenus.
   (d) *Argo* dedicated to Poseidon at Corinth.
9. Jason and Medea at Corinth: a Corinthian princess vs. a barbarian sorceress: opportunities for all.

10. The appropriate, yet ignoble, end of Jason; the *Argo* becomes a constellation.

11. Medea: a stop in Athens, then back to the East, where she becomes the ancestress of the Medes and lives nearer her grandfather, the Sun.

(For various accounts of the myth of the Argonauts, read Apollonius of Rhodes, *Argonautica;* Pindar, *Fourth Pythian Ode;* Euripides, *Medea;* Valerius Flaccus, *Argonautica.* Judith Anderson portrays Medea on a memorable record, Decca DLP 9000.)

B. Odysseus: the hero of Ithaca who became a legend in his own day. In many respects he was unlike the other heroes who fought at Troy; yet, for any difficult assignment, he was the man wanted or selected. Whether he was cunning or "sneaky," strong or "tricky," competent or "lucky," depends upon the reader's evaluation of Odysseus. Certainly, Odysseus always seemed to have the proper answer for any occasion; it may be a moot question to ask whether he or his patron-goddess, Athena, provided the answers. To judge Odysseus properly, one must read of his exploits in the *Iliad* and *Odyssey.* Here, we shall confine ourselves to his affairs after the Trojan War.

1. The journey home to Ithaca: many episodes parallel those found in the story of Jason.

   (a) The land of the Cicones and the gift of wine.

   (b) The land of the Lotus-Eaters (opium?).

   (c) The land of the Cyclops, Polyphemus; (the putting out of the eye of Polyphemus became one of the favorite subjects of Greek vase-painters, as some 10 extant vases attest); Odysseus, or "Noone," incurs the wrath of Poseidon.

   (d) The land of Aeolus, king of the winds.

   (e) The land of the Laestrygonians, whence one ship sails away.

   (f) The land of Aeaea, where Circe dwells; help from Hermes, and a happy visit: birth of Telegonus.

   (g) The land of the Cimmerians, where Odysseus learns more from Tiresias.

   (h) The land of the Sirens, the sweetest music this side of destruction.

   (i) The passage between Scylla and Charybdis.

(j) The land of the Sun's cattle; soon after, all but Odysseus are killed.

(k) The island Ogygia and the nymph Calypso; seven years with the wrong woman, and release on order of Zeus. Wrecked by Poseidon, but aided by Leucothea who gives him her veil, Odysseus floats on.

(l) The land of the Phaeacians: Nausicaa, and King Alcinous; the last leg of the journey home.

2. In Ithaca: recognition by Eumaeus, Telemachus, Argus (who dies from happiness and old age), and Eurycleia.

(a) Death of the suitors, beginning with Antinous.

(b) The recognition scene with Penelope, another of Homer's masterful husband-and-wife scenes.

3. The accidental death of Odysseus caused by Telegonus.

4. The curious finale: Telegonus marries Penelope, Telemachus marries Circe, and they all settle down in Aeaea.

(Two plays which further reveal the character of Odysseus are Sophocles' *Ajax* and *Philoctetes;* both plays also reveal the genius of Sophocles and should be read much more widely than they actually are.)

V. The Story of Atlantis: the original story of a complete country disappearing into the sea and becoming "lost" appears in Plato's *Timaeus.* This particular dialogue, the only one of Plato's works devoted to cosmology and natural science, may be dated about the year 422 or 421. The first part of the *Timaeus* is a recapitulation of Books 1-5 of the *Republic,* and the last part is a cosmological discourse delivered by Timaeus himself. While these two sections, especially the latter, have provoked serious scholarly discussions, the middle part of the work has appealed widely to authors, movie-makers, and day-dreamers ever since its composition; some have even taken Plato seriously and have tried to find the lost continent of Atlantis.

As Critias, one of the interlocutors, tells it, the story took place 9,000 years before the time of Solon (594 B. C.) . In that time the situation of Athens was analogous to that described in the first five books of the *Republic:* she was a small, agricultural community, filled with patriotism and simple morality. Soon, however, she had to encounter the united kings of Atlantis, an island lying beyond the Pillars of Heracles (Straits of Gibraltar). The Atlantians had already overrun Europe as far as Italy, and Africa as far as the border of Egypt. In the struggle Athens defeated the richer and more powerful kingdom. Shortly thereafter, the victorious Athens and the vanquished Atlantis were both overwhelmed in one day and night by an earthquake and tidal wave. The story, says Critias, survived in Egyptian records and came to Solon's attention when he visited Egypt.

The whole tale is presumably Plato's invention, although the materials for the tale may have been the alleged shallowness of the ocean just beyond the Pillars of Heracles, stories of sailors about islands in the Atlantic, and the earthquake and tidal wave which did hit the Greek coast in 373. The real emphasis of the story lay in the idea that a small, patriotic state could overcome an invader with far greater resources and knowledge of warfare. Clearly Plato seems to have been thinking of the real Athens and her real struggle against Persia; there, too, a rich and powerful kingdom was ingloriously beaten by a much smaller state, but one in which free people fought with a spirit unmatched by the aggressors. What Plato did, then, in this story was to project the events of the Persian Wars backward, magnify their scale, and point out the moral that the patriotism of a free society is more than a match for an enemy's larger numbers, greater wealth, and better engineering skill.

This bit of Platonic fantasy has stirred the imagination of many men throughout the centuries and may rightly be considered the basis for a Utopia which existed once, was lost, and will never be rediscovered. Had there been such a place, both Jason and Odysseus could have retired there and met better ends.

CHAPTER 7

Heroes and Their Exploits

If man has always dreamed of a better time and a better place to live and created his Utopias, he has also thought of a better man and created his heroes. Every society has had its own heroes, men with special endowments who left the world better than they had found it. The Sumerians had Gilgamesh, who, clad in his 50 pound armor and wielding his over-400 pound axe, killed the great snake and rescued the goddess Inanna. The Babylonians had Marduk, who, as a result of his exploits, became a god and then grew to be more powerful than his father, the god Enki. The Hebrews had Moses who led them out of Egypt, gave them the 10 Commandments, and then disappeared on Mt. Nebo in the land of Moab. The Greeks and the Romans had their share of heroes, many of whom fitted the pattern containing miracle, mystery, violence, and unusual death. (For a more detailed pattern, into which heroes of many lands are fitted, see Lord Raglan's *The Hero: A Study in Tradition, Myth, and Drama,* chapters xvi and xvii.)

I. Heracles, the Superman Turned God: by far the most popular and Pan-Hellenic hero, his origins may go back to the Mycenaean Age, i.e., the 15th century B. C., as Nilsson has argued in *The Mycenaean Origin of Greek Mythology.* Seltman, in *The Twelve Olympians,* suggests a double origin of Heracles, an older one in Mycenae and a later one in Boeotia (or Thebes). Whatever his beginning, the ending of Heracles' career is agreed upon by all: because of his heroic deeds, he became a full-fledged god on Olympus, married to Hebe, the daughter of Zeus and Hera. (The fact that he married his own half-sister pales before the fact that, by so doing, he was finally reconciled to Hera; besides, critics have not been too harsh on the two-fold status of Hera and Zeus as brother-sister and husband-wife.)

Before proceeding to a consideration of the feats of Heracles, it should be pointed out that the story of his conception and birth—his mother was Alcmena, and his father was Zeus in the form of Alcmena's husband, Amphitryon—has proved to be a most popular story for playwrights and composers. Some 56 plays and operas have been based on this theme, with such authors as Euripides, Plautus, Seneca, Molière, von Kleist, and Giraudoux having contributed to the number. For the complete list and an analysis of each work, see L. P. Shero, "Alcmena and Amphitryon in Ancient and Modern Drama," in *Transactions of the American Philological Association,* Vol. 87 (1956), 192-238. According to tradition, Alcmena was the last mortal woman visited by Zeus, since she had been selected to bear his most famous son, a son destined to be powerful enough to save both gods and men from destruction. From the very beginning, the life and career of Heracles merited Hera's unabated anger and anguish; she did succeed in delaying his birth, so it was perhaps with some justice that later his birthday was celebrated on the fourth day of each month.

Customarily, his feats are divided into three categories: the 12 Labors (*athloi*), the side-labors (*parerga*), and those before or after the Labors (*praxeis*). Just how and when the canon of 12 Labors was established is not known exactly, but some say that the grouping of those twelve which make up the "official" list first appeared on the temple of Zeus at Olympia. The first 6 Labors are often referred to as the Peloponnesian Group, since they take place in that area; the next 3 Labors are called the Eastern Group, and the last 3 the Western Group. We may conveniently list the Labors and then proceed to the *parerga* and *praxeis,* keeping in mind that the Labors were performed for King Eurystheus, were originally 10 in number, and resulted from Hera's enmity.

A. The 12 Labors (*athloi*)
1. Killing the Nemean Lion, which could not be killed by metal or stone: possible source of Heracles' garb and club.
2. Killing the multi-headed Hydra of Lerna, which could grow two new heads for each one lost; assistance

from Iolaus, son of Iphicles, the half twin-brother of Heracles; source of poison for Heracles' arrows which could cause death even from a scratch; this Labor discounted by Eurystheus.

3. Capture of the Erymanthian Boar.
4. Capture of the golden-horned Hind of Cerynea, which was sacred to Artemis.
5. Rout of the Stymphalian Birds, which had iron feathers and were sacred to Ares.
6. Cleaning of the Stables of Augeas, aided by the Alpheus and Peneus rivers; refused payment by Augeas; discounted by Eurystheus.
7. Capture of the Cretan Bull, which became the Bull of Marathon.
8. Capture of the man-eating mares of Thracian Diomedes.
9. Obtaining the girdle of Hippolyte, queen of the Amazons; Antiope taken as well and given to Theseus.
10. Driving of the cattle of Geryon from the far west to Greece.
11. Obtaining of the Golden Apples of the Hesperides, which were in the far west.
12. Capture of Cerberus, guardian of the Lower World.

B. *Parerga*

1. Brawl with the Centaurs, death of Pholus and Chiron, (3)
2. Killing of the Centaur Eurytion, (6)
3. Founded the city of Abdera, (8)
4. Rescue of Hesione at Troy; refused payment by Laomedon, (9)
5. Freed Crete of all wild beasts; out-wrestled Antaeus in Libya; killed Busiris and founded the city of 100-gated Thebes in Egypt; set up the Pillars of Heracles; aided by Zeus, drove off would-be rustlers in southern France; killed Cacus in Italy; killed Eryx in Sicily, (10)
6. Obtained advice from Nereus; killed Emathion in Ethiopia; freed Prometheus in Caucasus; on the way to the land of the Hyperboreans, killed Cycnus, a son of Ares, in Macedonia; tricked Atlas, (11)
7. Freed Theseus from the Chair of Forgetfulness. (12)

C. *Praxeis*
1. As a baby, killed 2 serpents sent by Hera.
2. Killed his music-teacher, Linus.
3. Killed the Thespian Lion; provided 51 sons for King Thespius by spending one night with 49 of the king's 50 daughters.
4. Relieved Thebes of paying tribute to Orchomenus and forced Minyans to pay twice as much tribute to Thebes.
5. Killed wife Megara and sons in madness sent by Hera; ordered to undertake Labors for Eurystheus.
6. Established the Olympic Games in honor of Zeus and won every event.
7. Sailed with the Argonauts, lost Hylas, and didn't go on.
8. Restored Alcestis from the Lower World, having wrestled Hades (or Thanatos).
9. Killed Iphitus in madness sent by Hera.
10. Served Queen Omphale in Lydia as a slave: captured the Cercopes; killed Syleus, a master vine-pruner.
11. Attacked King Laomedon of Troy; killed Laomedon and all but one son, Priam.
12. Aided the Olympians vs. the Giants.
13. Killed Augeas for non-payment of salary.
14. Killed Neleus and all but one son, Nestor.
15. Out-wrestled river-god Achelous for Deianira: cornucopia.
16. Killed Nessus, who tried to violate Deianira.
17. Killed Amyntor and seized his daughter by force; killed Eurytus and seized his daughter Iole.
18. Died, ironically, as a result of his own poisoned arrow, via the blood of the centaur, Nessus.
19. Disappeared as funeral pyre burned, and was taken to Olympus.
20. Became a god, and married Hebe.

Other, non-categorized activities of Heracles included his being trained in the arts and sciences by expert teachers, his being initiated into the Eleusinian Mysteries, and his apparent attempt to populate the whole earth with his sons. (Only one reference, in Euripides, mentions a daughter.) His character may have left something to be desired, but after all, he was a super-man, fond of the usual man's pleasures, yet surpassing the usual man's indulgence in wine, women, and battle. There remains some difficulty in reconciling Heracles' desire to satisfy his appetites and the story told by Xenophon (*Memorabilia* 2.1) of his choice between Pleasure and Virtue; in the story he chose Virtue, who promised a hard life but one which would bring him immortality. To be sure, his life was not easy, despite the obvious pleasures, and his deification may have been justly earned by his having ridded the world of wild beasts and villains. Perhaps he did not exemplify the two caveats, "Know Thyself" and "Nothing in Excess:" he apparently didn't know his own strength or drinking capacity at times, often exhibited a superiority complex, and did nothing in excess, unless he enjoyed it greatly. Still, the better elements of the hero's character more than compensated for his shortcomings and insured his acceptance among the gods. (Cf. Lucretius, *De Rerum Natura* 5, who compares Heracles' ridding the world of beasts with the ordinary man's inability to rid himself of such "beasts" as pride, lust, and boredom.) Finally, we may note that Heracles did become a patron saint among the Stoics, who were inclined to overlook or forget any bad habits of the hero-god.

II. Other heroes, almost gods: each tended to be closely associated with a particular city or locale, and most reveal many elements of the heroic pattern: (e.g. miraculous birth, attempts on their life at an early age, magnificent exploits, often assisted by gods, and unusual death).

 A. Theseus: associated with Athens, often credited with being the organizer of that city, its first king, and the man who set it upon the path of civilization. Son of Aegeus (or Poseidon) and Aethra, he grew up in Troezen; on his way from Troezen to Athens occurred the 6 Labors assigned to him:

   1. Killed Periphetes with his own bronze club and kept the club for future use; near Epidaurus.
   2. Killed Sinis, the pine-bender, in his own fashion; at the Isthmus of Corinth; fathered Melanippus by Perigune, daughter of Sinis.
   3. Killed the Sow of Crommyon, named Phaea, who may have been a female robber.
   4. Killed Sciron by throwing him off his own cliff; near

Megara.

5. Killed Cercyon by applying wrestling techniques, (rather than sheer strength), for the first time in history.
6. Killed Procrustes by fitting to his own bed; in Attica, near Athens.

Having been purified for these deaths by the sons of Phytalus, Theseus arrived in Athens, where his father and step-mother received him. As a result of the jealousy of his step-mother, Medea, Theseus had to capture the Bull of Marathon, and, soon thereafter, he narrowly avoided death by poison she prepared for him. Reunited with Aegeus, and with Medea gone, Theseus was ready for further adventures:

1. Killing of the Minotaur, in Crete; assisted and loved by Adriadne; desertion of Ariadne, and mistaken death of Aegeus; Theseus becomes king of Athens.
2. Assisted Oedipus in his last days; retrieved bodies of the leaders of the Seven Against Thebes.
3. War with Amazons: by Antiope, or Hippolyte, he had son, Hippolytus.
4. Participated in struggle of Lapiths vs. Centaurs at the marriage of Pirithous and Hippodamia.
5. With Pirithous, he stole Helen and hid her away and tried to steal Persephone: both seated in Chairs of Forgetfulness, but Theseus freed by Heracles.
6. His wife, Phaedra, rebuffed by Hippolytus, made false accusations and hanged herself; death, by mistake, of Hippolytus (who, in one story, was revived by Asclepius).
7. Banished from Athens, retired to Scyros, where King Lycomedes pushed him off a cliff to his death; later, Cimon of Athens recovered his body and reburied it in Athens.

Theseus was usually listed among the Argonauts and the hunters of the Calydonian Boar; he was considered important enough to have a biography included in the *Lives* by Plutarch. Many other deeds were ascribed to him, and a good number of those closely paralleled adventures of Heracles. The more significant of these were connected with Athens, such as incorporating the city, giving it a constitution, and insuring its place of honor at the Isthmian Games, (which some say he founded to worship Poseidon). His associations with Athens were compatible with the fact that he was always close to the god Apollo.

B. Perseus: grandson of Acrisius, king of Argos; son of Zeus (as a shower of gold) and Danaë; attempt upon lives of mother and son failed, as the chest carried them safely over the waves to Seriphus, where Polydectes ruled. Polydectes, filled with desire for Danaë, arranged an exciting adventure for Perseus: killing the Gorgon, Medusa. Equipped by the gods, Perseus completed the mission and went on to others:

1. Killed Medusa, from whose blood sprang Pegasus and serpents.
2. Turned Atlas to stone.
3. Rescued and married Andromeda, after killing the dragon; (how coral came to be).
4. Turned Phineus and his followers to stone.
5. Petrified Polydectes and put Dictys on throne of Seriphus.
6. Took part in games at Larissa, Thessaly, and accidentally killed grandfather Acrisius with discus.
7. Became king of Tiryns and gave Medusa's head to Athena, who put it on her shield.
8. Perhaps founded Mycenae, after a lonely mushroom had given him food and drink; or
8. (a) Withdrew to Asia, where his son ruled and gave name to Persians.

C. Bellerophon: a descendant of Sisyphus, he could be expected to have troubles; of doubtful parentage, his original name was Hipponous. Killed Bellerus, (whence Bellerophon), killed brother accidentally, went from Corinth to Argos, from bad to no better. There false accusations by the king's wife, Anteia (or Sthenoboea), caused King Proteus to send Bellerophon for punishment to Iobates, king of Lycia and father of Anteia (or Sthenoboea). Hence, these adventures:

1. Astride Pegasus, killed the Chimaera, a lion-goat-serpent trimonster; note earlier assistance of Athena.
2. Defeated the Solymi.
3. Fought the Amazons.
4. Killed the ambuscading warriors of Iobates; aid from Poseidon.
5. Married a daughter of Iobates, who gave this bless-

ing: "If you can't lick 'em, join 'em!" Philonoë and Bellerophon had three children, the most famous of whom was Laodomia, who, by Zeus, became mother of Sarpedon.

6. On Pegasus, tried to fly to Olympus; Zeus caused Pegasus to throw off Bellerophon who crashed to earth and thereafter was lame and blind; two of his children died, and he simply "wandered away, shunning the paths of men" (Homer, *Iliad* 6).

D. Dioscuri ("Sons of Zeus") : Castor and Polydeuces (Pollux) : though according to traditions the twin sons of Leda and Zeus, some accounts gave her husband Tyndareus as the father of Castor (and Clytemnestra) and Zeus as the father of Polydeuces (and Helen). Closely associated with Sparta, Castor was famous as a horseman and Polydeuces as a boxer. They did not figure largely in many stories:

1. Sailed with the Argonauts: Polydeuces vs. Amycus.
2. Participated in the Calydonian Boar Hunt.
3. Helped Peleus capture Iolcus and Cretheis, the wife of Acastus who had falsely accused Peleus of improper advances.
4. Rescued their sister Helen, who had been hidden away by Theseus and Pirithous.
5. Affairs with Idas and Lynceus: theft of prospective brides; reconciliation; theft of cattle and fall-out of thieves; battle in which Idas killed Castor, Polydeuces killed Lynceus, and Zeus killed Idas; Zeus agreed to let Castor and Polydeuces share the latter's immortality: thus, they alternate in Hades and on earth or Olympus, or (as Spartans said) Polydeuces became the Morning Star and Castor the Evening Star. Another version stated that Zeus put both men in the heavens as the constellation, Gemini.

As heroes, Castor and Polydeuces were especially favored by warriors and sea-farers. Among the Romans, the twins were held in great esteem, as evidenced by the quite common expletives, *mecastor* and *edopol* (see the plays of Plautus and Terence, for example). Their temple in Rome was built, in fulfillment of a vow, soon after the Battle of Lake Regillus in 496 B. C.; rebuilt by Tiberius in 6 A. D., remains of the temple still stand.

E. The Calydonian Boar Hunt: all the famous heroes assembled to hunt down the boar sent to ravage Calydon by Artemis, because King Oeneus forgot to sacrifice to her. Focus of the story settled on Meleager, fated to live as long as a certain fire-brand was not burned up, and Atalanta, object of Meleager's love. Atalanta first wounded the boar, and Meleager killed it; in a quarrel over whether the boar's hide and head should be given to Atalanta, Meleager killed his two uncles. After hearing the news of her brother's death, Althea, Meleager's mother, put the certain fire-brand in the flames to be consumed. Meleager's life flickered out, and Althea committed suicide. (This version according to Ovid, *Metamorphoses* 8).

A quite different version was told by Homer, *Iliad* 9: in a fierce struggle vs. the Curetes, Meleager was at last persuaded to save the city, Calydon; his lateness, however, cost him the many rewards earlier promised him. (This story was detailed by old Phoenix in his attempt to persuade Achilles to return to the Trojan War).

F. Asclepius: son of Apollo and Coronis. As suggested by W. K. C. Guthrie, in *The Greeks and Their Gods,* the position of Asclepius, as a hero or as a god, is difficult to determine. Not mentioned by Hesiod, but referred to by Homer (*Iliad* 4.193), he had a double birth, similar to Dionysus, in some accounts. Taught by Chiron, Apollo, and possibly Athena, Asclepius became famous as a physician and healer. A familiar story said that Asclepius restored the dead Hippolytus to life yet was killed by Zeus for over-stepping his powers.

His most famous shrine was at Epidaurus, the ancient Lourdes, where cures were effected with the aid of snakes. The island Cos contained a shrine to him, and produced a great physician of its own, Hippocrates. Brought to Rome in the early 3rd century B. C., his shrine was located on the island in the Tiber River; the same island today houses a hospital, verifying the island's efficacy as a place of healing.

G. Romulus and Remus: though heroes of Rome, many elements of their careers closely resemble Greek and Near Eastern stories:

1. Born of Rhea Silvia, who had been made a virgin-priestess by her uncle Amulius, and Mars.
2. Aumulius' plan to kill the babes thwarted by his agent's fear of water.
3. Suckled by a she-wolf, discovered and reared by Faustulus and his wife.
4. In young manhood, their exploits made them prototypes of Robin Hood; Remus captured.
5. Rescue by Romulus, death of Amulius and restoration of Numitor to kingship of Alba Longa.
6. Decision to found city where, as babes in the basket, they had come to rest along Tiber's shore: omens favored Remus by time but Romulus by number as nominal founder.
7. Romulus, who was short of a sense of humor, killed Remus, who was not a good loser.
8. As Rome's first king, Romulus ruled some 40 years; his most publicized act, (and apparently most necessary act), was to acquire wives for his men: rape of the Sabine women; established laws and some religious rites.
9. Disappearance of Romulus in a thunderstorm; Romans convinced he had been taken to join the gods.
10. Given the name Quirinus and his own college of priests as a god.

The most detailed account of the careers of Romulus and Remus is that of Livy, *Ab Urbe Condita* 1.

The reader is reminded again that the above list is by no means exhaustive or complete. Local heroes abounded throughout the ancient lands, as did local gods. As local heroes, worshipped with shrines, sacrifices, and rites, these figures occupied a role similar to that of saints in the Christian church. Whether heroes were born or made, whether their origins lays in custom and ritual or in history, whether any contemporary records vouched for the hero's life and acts—these and like questions concern the scholars, but they were not important to those who believed the tradition transmitted to them by their ancestors. St. Augustine's suggestion, *"Crede ut intelligas"* ("Believe that you may know") seems most appropriate in the consideration of heroes and hero-gods.

CHAPTER 8
Two Bronze Age Wars

No two cities so dominated mythology with their stories of legendary men and women, gods and demi-gods as did Thebes and Troy. Legends surrounding these cities provided much rich material for bards, epic poets, and tragedians. Both Thebes and Troy could boast of founders descended from powerful gods, Poseidon and Zeus respectively; the same two gods played important roles in the development of the cities: Zeus' carrying off Europa led to Cadmus' following out the orders of the oracle and founding Thebes, and Poseidon helped in the building of the walls of Troy as punishment meted out by Zeus. (Read Livy, *Preface* of the *Ab Urbe Condita,* for his views on the desire of cities to claim origins from the gods.)

Further, both cities enjoyed great historical significance: the position of Thebes at the time of the beginning of the Peloponnesian War was vividly related by Thucydides; her period of hegemony came after Sparta and Athens had exhausted themselves in the war, when Epaminondas led her forces in the 4th century. As for Troy, archaeologists have done much to confirm Homer's tale and to prove that the site of Troy was a strategic one, as the many cities built in succession on the site suggest. Perhaps, as Horace pointed out, there were brave men before Agamemnon; but, at least, we know him and his assault on Troy, just as we know old Tiresias, whose life at Thebes spanned seven generations of men. These famous men, along with their contemporaries, lived and died in the period known as the Bronze Age, as Homer himself attested. Reading histories of those cities and their heroes, we can only be happy that a Homer did come along to record for us the stories of that Age, which came to a close in the 12th century B. C. Still greater appreciation, both of the cities and their heroes and of those writers who later told their tales, may be gained by reading appropriate works in Greek and Roman epic and drama.

I. **The Theban Cycle: the following genealogical chart will supply the information needed to trace through the ruling line:**

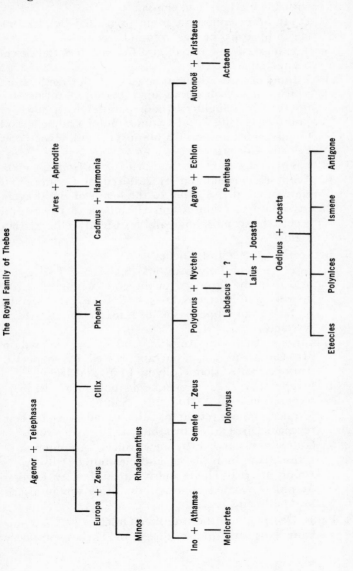

The Royal Family of Thebes

A. The Story of Cadmus
   1. Carrying off of Europa by Zeus, which led to Agenor's demand of his sons to find Europa; Cadmus set out with his mother, Telephassa.
   2. Death of Telephassa; Cadmus consulted Delphic oracle and learned he was to found a new city.
   3. The marked cow rested, and Cadmus had the site of his new city.
   4. Killing of Ares' dragon; sowing of the teeth, from which armed men sprang up (*Spartoi*) ; 5 survive the internecine slaughter, (note parallel with story of Jason in Colchis), aid Cadmus build Cadmeia, and found noble families: Chthonius, Echion, Hyperenor, Pelorus, Udaeus.
   5. His marriage to Harmonia; bridal gifts from the gods.
   6. Troubles encountered by children of Cadmus and Harmonia; all traceable to the death of the dragon.
   7. Departure of Cadmus and Harmonia to Illyria and eventual metamorphoses and transferal to the Elysian Fields.

B. Between Cadmeia and Thebes
   1. After rule of Polydorus and Labdacus, Lycus succeeded to the throne with the good wishes of Dirce, his wife, and Nyctaeus, loved by Zeus; to escape wrath of father and uncle, she fled to Sicyon; death of Nyctaeus.
   3. Antiope's twin sons, Amphion and Zethus, exposed on Mt. Cithaeron but saved and reared by shepherd; Antiope treated shamefully by Lycus and Dirce.
   4. Escape of Antiope to shepherd's house (by chance) ; recognition scene: "Mother!"; "Sons!"
   5. Mother and sons return to Cadmeia and sweep to their revenge: Dirce killed by a bull, Lycus by a sword.
   6. Cadmeia expanded by new rulers, Amphion and Zethus; Amphion played music to build walls by.
   7. Zethus married Thebe and renamed the city Thebes; Amphion married Niobe, whose pride was punished by Apollo and Artemis.

C. Laius, Oedipus, and the Infallible Oracle
   1. Laius king, and Jocasta queen, of Thebes: prophecy

of a son who would kill his father and marry his mother.

2. Son born and exposed on Mt. Cithaeron; found by shepherd and taken to King Polybus of Corinth.

3. Oedipus heard that Polybus was not real father and went to Delphi to discover the truth: told that he would kill his father and marry his mother, he headed from "home" to Thebes.

4. Meeting and fight at a cross-roads: a hot-headed old man killed by a hot-headed young man who continued walking to Thebes.

5. Solving the riddle of the Sphinx by giving proper answer, "man," Oedipus was rewarded with kingship and queen.

6. Several years and four children later, Oedipus insisted on finding an answer for the plague which had hit Thebes.

7. Tiresias' words fulfilled: Jocasta killed self, Oedipus blinded self, left Thebes, then left the sight of men at Colonus.

(Note that Oedipus fits many of the requirements of a hero; read Sophocles' magnificent plays concerned with Oedipus and his fate: *Oedipus Tyrannus* and *Oedipus at Colonus*.)

D. The Seven Against Thebes

1. After the interregnum of Creon, Eteocles and Polynices, sons of Oedipus and Jocasta, agreed to rule Thebes alternately for a year.

2. Eteocles liked ruling and refused to let Polynices into power; Polynices persuaded his father-in-law, King Adrastus of Argos, to lead an army vs. Thebes.

3. Bribing Eriphyle with the golden necklace of Harmonia, Polynices persuaded Eriphyle to persuade Amphiaraus, a famous seer, to join in the expedition.

4. Army marshalled under 7 leaders: Polynices, Adrastus, Amphiaraus, Tydeus, Capaneus, Hippomedon, Parthenopaeus (7 leaders, one for each gate of Thebes).

5. On the road to Thebes: death of Opheltes at Nemea and founding of the Nemean Games; the unsuccessful embassy, and successful fight, of Tydeus.

6. Menoeceus of Thebes killed himself to insure victory of Thebes, as the army of the 7 attack.

7. Capaneus, too boastful, killed by Zeus; Hippomedon
was killed by Ismarus; Parthenopaeus by Pericly-
menus, a son of Poseidon; Tydeus and Melanippus
killed each other; Polynices and Eteocles killed each
other; Amphiaraus, chariot and all, swallowed up in a
chasm created by Zeus; Adrastus alone escaped, as the
expedition failed.

(Read Aeschylus, *The Seven Against Thebes*, and Euripides,
The Suppliants, to compare the views of the women in Thebes
before the battle and the views of the women outside of Thebes
after the battle. Statius' epic poem, the *Thebaid*, covers much
the same ground as the play of Aeschylus.)

After the first unsuccessful expedition, Creon became king of
Thebes and at once ran into trouble (see Sophocles, *Antigone*).
The bodies of the attackers were recovered by their widows
and/or Theseus; Evadne, wife of Capaneus, killed herself on
her husband's pyre, in order to be with him in death. An interlude of 10 years occurred, while plans were being made by the
sons of the 7 who had first attacked Thebes.

E. The Epigoni ("After-born")

1. Alcmaeon made leader as a result of his mother's
(Eriphyle) being bribed by Thersander, son of Polynices; on this occasion, the robe of Harmonia was too
much for Eriphyle to resist.

2. Leaders of the Epigoni: Alcmaeon, and Amphilochus
(?), (sons of Amphiaraus); Aegialeus (son of Adrastus); Diomedes (son of Tydeus); Promachus (son of
Parthenopaeus); Sthenelus (son of Capaneus); Thersander (son of Polynices); Euryalus (son of Mecis-
teus), or Polydorus (son of Hippomedon). Adrastus,
though old, accompanied the forces.

3. Only Aegialeus, son of Adrastus, was killed; Adrastus
died of grief, and Thebes fell—all as predicted by
Tiresias.

4. Alcmaeon returned to Argos, discovered the bribes,
killed his mother, and was pursued by the Furies.
Purified by King Phegeus, married Arsinoë, and gave
her the cursed robe and necklace of Harmonia. Furies
reappeared, and Alcmaeon went to river-god Achelous,
who purified him and give him Calirrhoë in marriage.
Calirrhoë desired the robe and necklace: deceit, and

death of Alcmaeon by sons of Phegeus; robe and necklace deposited at Delphi (from where, Pausanias said, they were stolen in the 4th century B. C.).

II. The Trojan Cycle: two genealogical charts present figures of importance in the tale of Troy:

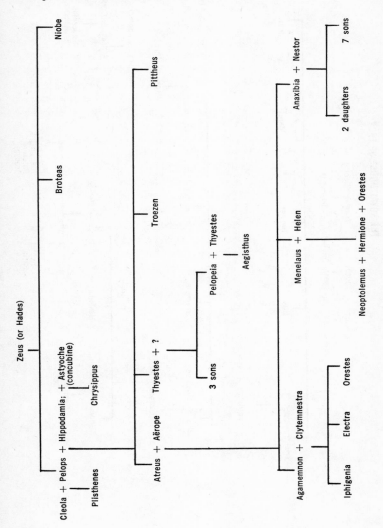

THE ROYAL HOUSE OF TROY

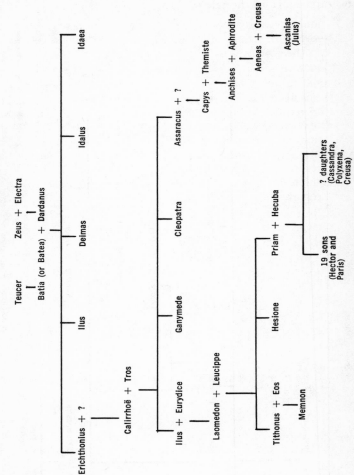

The Greek belief that sin begets sin is nowhere better illustrated than in the House of Atreus. The line of sin began with Tantalus and continued on through Orestes, who was, at last, purified completely:

A. Tantalus: to test omniscience of the gods, cooked and served up to the gods his own son, Pelops; Pelops restored and given ivory shoulder to replace the one eaten by sorrowing Demeter; Tantalus given lasting punishment in the Lower World.

B. Pelops: at Elis won Hippodamia as his wife by defeating her father, Oenomaus, in a chariot-race; he won by bribing Myrtilus, a son of Hermes and driver for Oenomaus, to remove an axle pin. Oenomaus was killed, and, when Myrtilus asked for his promised pay, he was taken on the first "one-way ride"; as he fell to his death, he put a curse upon the house of Pelops. Purified·by Hephaestus and reconciled with Hermes, Pelops took over the kingdom ruled by Oenomaus; subsequently, the whole area was renamed Peloponnesus in his honor.

C. Broteas: refused to worship Artemis and boasted that not even fire could harm him; driven mad by Artemis, he threw himself into a fire and perished.

D. Niobe: boasted of her children until relieved of them by Apollo and Artemis; she was transformed into a continually weeping rock.

E. Hippodamia: killed Chrysippus, fearing Pelops might leave kingdom to him.

F. Atreus, Aërope, Thyestes, and children:
   1. After death of Chrysippus, Atreus went to Mycenae where he became king and married Aërope.
   2. Thyestes won love of Aërope; together they seized power.
   3. Atreus, with aid of Zeus, caused the sun to reverse its path and regained throne: Thyestes was banished, and Aërope was flung into the sea.
   4. Discovering that Thyestes had been responsible for death of Plisthenes, Atreus lured him to Mycenae and served him his sons for dinner; Thyestes told the truth, went into exile uttering a curse against Atreus.
   5. To remove a plague, Atreus sought to bring back

Thyestes; in Sicyon, he met and fell in love with, and married Pelopeia who was pregnant by her own father.

6. Aegisthus, son of Thyestes and Pelopeia, born and exposed by mother; found and brought to Atreus, he is reared as the son of Atreus.

7. Thyestes later brought back to Mycenae by Atreus and put into prison; Atreus ordered his "son" to kill the prisoner: recognition of father and son who then kill Atreus; suicide of Pelopeia after learning truth.

8. Agamemnon and Menelaus fled, as Thyestes took over Mycenae; after his death, they returned, aided by their father-in-law Tyndareus, king of Sparta.

(It may be observed in passing that this grim and horrible legend concerning the rule of Mycenae was apparently not known by Homer or Hesiod; at least, neither made reference to it. For elaborations on the story, see Aeschylus, *Agamemnon*, Euripides, *Electra* and *Orestes*, and Seneca, *Thyestes*.)

9. To obtain favorable winds to Troy, Agamemnon sacrificed his daughter, Iphigenia: Interlude of War.

10. Back home after the war, Agamemnon and his current concubine, Cassandra, were killed by Clytemnestra and Aegisthus.

11. Return of Orestes, who avenged his father by killing his mother and Aegisthus (8 years after death of Agamemnon).

12. Orestes pursued by Furies, purified in vain, but finally acquitted in a trial: End of the Curse.

(For events just listed, read Aeschylus, *Choëphoroe,* and Sophocles *Electra,* as well as those cited between 8 and 9 above; for a variant concerning the fate of Iphigenia, see Euripides, *Iphigenia at Aulis* and *Iphigenia among the Taurians.*)

III. The point at which the two above genealogies met was, of course, the Trojan War. Since most authorities agree that the Trojan Epic Cycle (as it came to be called) was post-Homeric and intended to present a full account of the war, we may assume that the *Iliad* and *Odyssey* were the original focal points around which the other episodes were fitted. Before seeing the war *in toto,* therefore, let us consider first the two works of Homer; then we can fit those into the total pattern with rèsumès, as we know them, of the other poems which constituted the Trojan Cycle. Finally, we shall trace the meta-morphosis of Troy into Rome, according to Virgil's *Aeneid*.

A. The *Iliad* of Homer: The Wrath of Achilles, events of some 47-49 days in the 10th year of the Trojan War.

1. To stop the plague among the Greeks, Agamemnon reluctantly sends back Chryseis to her father, a priest of Apollo. A replacement is found, after a stormy assembly session, in Briseis, who is transferred from the tent of Achilles to that of Agamemnon. Achilles, therefore, and his Myrmidons withdraw from battle, and the Greek army is badly battered by the Trojans (Books 1-8).

2. Agamemnon dispatches Odysseus, Ajax, and Phoenix to the tent of Achilles, promising him rich rewards if he will return to action: Achilles replies that (1) he will go home the next day, (2) that on the next day he will consider going home, and (3) that he will not fight until the Trojans have set fire to the Greek ships (Book 9).

3. After a night during which Diomedes and Odysseus, spying on the Trojans, kill Dolon, spying on the Greeks, and take the horses of Rhesus, a furious struggle sees the wounding of many stout Greeks and the onslaught of the Trojans, led by Hector, against the Greek camp. Poseidon slips aid to the Greeks, until Zeus orders him out of action in the fighting. Patroclus gains permission to wear Achilles' armor and lead Myrmidons vs. the Trojans; ignoring the advice of Achilles, however, Patroclus goes too far and is killed by Hector and Apollo (Books 10-17).

4. Achilles, bent only on avenging the death of Patroclus, is reconciled with Agamemnon, puts on resplendent new armor made by Hephaestus, and re-enters the battle. In contrast to the rather meaningless combat of the gods, the mortals engage fiercely, with Achilles finally confronting Hector. Achilles kills Hector and, exulting in his victory, drags the body around and around, at last taking it to his tent (Books 18-22).

5. After the shade of Patroclus reminds Achilles of his funerary obligations and those are discharged, King Priam of Troy, guided safely by Hermes, comes to

Achilles' tent to recover the body of Hector; Achilles relents, and the poem ends with the laments of the women over Hector's body (Books 22-24).

B. The *Odyssey* of Homer: The Wanderings of Odysseus, events which delayed his homecoming to Ithaca for 10 years.

1. Telemachus is urged by the gods to search for his father Odysseus and visits Pylos and Lacedaemon. Meanwhile, the suitors of Penelope in Ithaca plot death for Telemachus (Books 1-4).

2. Calypso, at Zeus' bidding, helps Odysseus leave her land, but Poseidon wrecks his ship; relying on the veil of Leucothea, Odysseus, after three days, reaches the land of Phaeacia. Kindly received there, he recounts to his hosts his past wanderings (Books 5-12). (See Chapter 6, IV.B above for a detailed account of his adventures.)

3. Taken to Ithaca by a ship of the Phaeacians, Odysseus is given disguise as a beggar, reveals his identity to his returned son Telemachus; together, they plan the overthrow of the suitors (Books 13-16).

4. In his beggar's disguise, Odysseus arrives in his palace, is greeted by his old dog Argus (who drops dead), and becomes an object of humor and scorn to the suitors; meanwhile, Telemachus removes the arms of the suitors, and Penelope resolves on the morrow to select a new husband from among the suitors by marrying whoever can string the bow of Odysseus and shoot an arrow through the 12 axes. Eurycleia recognizes Odysseus by a scar on his foot (Books 17-20).

5. The suitors are shot down, and Odysseus and Penelope are reunited; a budding war between Odysseus, Laertes and followers and relatives of the slain suitors is abruptly halted by Zeus, and peace between the groups is established (Books 20-24).

With these two poems as the core, we may briefly indicate the contents, as we know them, of the other poems which were composed to complete the Trojan Cycle:

A. *Cypria,* by Stasinos (?): Eris and the golden apple; the first beauty contest and the judgment of Paris; abduction of Helen, and plans of Greeks; the assembly at Aulis and near sacrifice of Iphigenia; the abandoning of Philoctetes with the bow and arrows of Heracles; arrival at Troy, and death of Palamedes who had incurred the anger of Odysseus by showing that Odysseus had been the first "draft-dodger."

B. *Iliad.*

C. *Aethiopis,* by Arctinus: arrival of Penthesileia and the Amazons to fight with Troy; Achilles kills her and then a fellow-Greek, Thersites, who mocked his victory over a woman; Achilles, purified of guilt, kills Memnon of Ethiopia, but then is killed by Paris and Apollo; funeral of Achilles, and contest for his arms between Odysseus and Ajax; suicide of Ajax.

D. *Little Iliad,* by Lesches: contest for arms of Achilles; arrival of Neoptolemus (or Pyrrhus), son of Achilles at Troy; fetching to Troy of Philoctetes with arms of Heracles; death of Paris by Philoctetes' arrow.

E. *Sack of Ilium,* by Arctinus: the Wooden Horse episode: departure from Troy of Aeneas; Sinon's success with the Trojans, and the capture of Troy; death of Polyxena and Astyanax, and dividing of women and other booty; Greeks depart from Troy.

F. *Nostoi* ("Returns"), by Hagias: returns to their homeland by Neoptolemus, Calchas, Nestor, Diomedes, Menelaus and Agamemnon; death of Agamemnon.

G. *Odyssey.*

H. *Telegonia,* by Eugammon: events after the death of the suitors: death of Odysseus; marriages of Telemachus and Circe, and of Telegonus and Penelope; all retire to Circe's island, where presumably they lived happily ever after.

The tale of Troy is not complete until the wanderings and wars of Aeneas have been recounted, since, because of these, the greatest metamorphosis of all took place, *viz.,* the Trojan race into the Roman race. This transformation is dramatically told by Ovid in the *Metamorphoses* (Books 10-15) and by Virgil in the *Aeneid.* The latter work may be conveniently synopsized here for in the *Aeneid* we find best expressed the fullest statement of Roman aims and capabilities, as well as the description of how old Troy became in time new Rome.

1. As the result of a storm caused by Juno, Aeneas and his men are scattered over the sea in this, the seventh year of

their wandering attempt to settle in their destined Italy; blown to Africa, Aeneas, assisted by his disguised mother, Venus, makes his way into Carthage where he is welcomed by Queen Dido and the Carthaginians; she tells Aeneas of how she came to found this new city, and he, in turn, tells her and assembled hosts of his difficulties during and after the fall of Troy (Books 1-3).

2. After delaying in Carthage, Aeneas is reminded by Jupiter, through Mercury, that he must fulfill his duty to himself and others and sail on to Italy; distraught at her lover's departure, Dido commits suicide, after putting a curse upon future Rome-Carthage relations. A stop-over in Sicily allows the Trojans to celebrate the anniversary of Anchises' death, after which they move to the shore of Italy (Books 4-5).

3. A visit to the Sibyl at Cumae and fulfillment of three prerequisites give Aeneas the privilege of visiting the Lower World to talk with his father Anchises (See Chapter 5, 3.D above); Anchises reveals the future heroes and destiny of Rome, pointing out Rome's mission of world-rule (Book 6).

4. Juno stirs up hatred among the Italians, and soon thereafter, the Trojans are faced with war; Turnus provides the leadership of the Italians, with Mezentius and Camilla other notable warriors; the eventual, and final, showdown between Aeneas and Turnus occurs, with Aeneas triumphing; here the *Aeneid* ends, though we know that Aeneas will marry Lavinia, the Latin princess, and that the Trojan line will inter-marry with Italians and thus be re-established in its new homeland.

The figure of Aeneas was, of course, the dominating one in the poem; more important than his actions, however, were his motives and character, all of which were summed up in the epithet, *pius.* This word denoted the sense of manifold duty— to one's gods, one's country, one's family and oneself. Aeneas quite clearly portrayed the quality as he left burning Troy, carrying his country's gods in one hand, leading his son Ascanius by the other hand, and carrying his father Anchises on his shoulders. *Pius Aeneas* was to become the standard by which later Romans could be compared and a model to all future generations. The epithet, *pius,* was applied sparingly in the

Roman Republic; the emperor Antoninus (138-161 A. D.) was given *pius* as a cognomen in recognition of his admirable traits. At about the same time, c. 140-155 A. D., the bishop of Rome took Pius I as his official name; so, simultaneously, the head of the temporal state and the (then questionable) head of the Christian church had the same appellation. About 1,000 years later, Enea Sylvio de Piccolomini was elected bishop of Rome and ruled the church as Pope Pius II; the most recent Pius was Eugenio Pacelli, who was the head of the Roman Catholic Church as Pope Pius XII from 1939 to 1958.

Thus, with the rise of Rome attested by Virgil and Ovid, the prophecy of Helenus to the departing Aeneas was fulfilled: "Troy will not entirely perish as long as you live . . . you will carry Troy to a land more friendly than your native land . . . I see that a better Troy is destined, a city greater than any which has existed, exists now, or will exist in the future." (Ovid, *Metamorphoses,* Book 15) . Should not, then, "Rome Eternal" be more properly called "Troy Eternal"?

CHAPTER 9

Myths of Love and Other Tales

In this chapter will be considered many myths which have love as their basic theme; in most cases, love is the passion felt by one human being for another, rather than love in the cosmic sense. At the conclusion of the chapter, we shall see how Ovid made use of love in both senses and in a patriotic sense as well. For the sake of convenience, headings will indicate the type of love stories told within each section:

A. Simple Love Stories, with tragic or happy endings

1. Pyramus and Thisbe: death of the lovers, and the fruit of the mulberry tree turns from white to red (Ovid, *Metamorphoses* 4; cf. *Romeo and Juliet*).

2. Hero and Leander: both drown in the Hellespont (Ovid, *Heroides* 18 and 19; cf. Marlowe's *Hero and Leander*).

3. Demophon and Phyllis: in most versions, Phyllis committed suicide by hanging; in one version, Demophon was subsequently killed after a curse put upon him by Phyllis (Ovid, *Heroides* 2).

4. Iphis and Ianthe: a happy ending provided by Isis who made a father and a wife happy (Ovid, *Metamorphoses* 9).

5. Iphis and Anaxarete: a stone-hearted girl, responsible for a lover's suicide, becomes all stone as Venus punishes her (Ovid, *Metamorphoses* 14).

6. Acontius and Cydippe: another inscribed apple story, but with a happy ending (Ovid, *Heroides* 20 and 21).

7. Cephalus and Procris: suspicion and distrust lead to accidental death of Procris (Ovid, *Metamorphoses* 7).

8. Dido and Aeneas: suicide for Dido and on-to-Italy for Aeneas (Virgil, *Aeneid* 6, and Ovid, *Heroides* 7).

9. Ceyx and Alcyone: Morpheus tells Alcyone of the fate of Ceyx, who joins her husband in death (Ovid, *Metamorphoses* 11) .

10. Ariadne and Theseus: assistance, deliverance, and abandonment on Naxos; suicide of Ariadne, or rescue by Dionysus (Ovid, *Heroides* 10) .

11. Hypermnestra and Lynceus: disobedience of father's command brings happiness to wife and husband (Ovid, *Heroides* 14.)

12. Deianira and Heracles: accidental death caused by love and jealousy (Sophocles, *Women of Trachis (Trachiniae)*, and Ovid, *Heroides* 9) .

13. Orpheus and Eurydice: music charms Pluto, but a backward glance cost Orpheus his bride (Ovid, *Metamorphoses* 10 and 11) .

14. Baucis and Philemon: equal in life and in death (Ovid, *Metamorphoses* 8) .

15. Pygmalion: a statue becomes live, and the created one becomes a creator (Ovid, *Metamorphoses* 10) .

B. Triangle stories: two women and one man

1. Oenone, Paris, and Helen: the grass is always greener in another's yard (Ovid, *Heroides* 5, 16, 17) .

2. Clytemnestra, Agamemnon, and Cassandra: death of Cassandra but frosting on the cake to Clytemnestra (Aeschylus, *Agamemnon*) .

3. Andromache, Neoptolemus (Pyrrhus) , and Hermione hoped to have Andromache killed, but the people of Delphi, or Peleus, stopped her.

4. Medea, Jason, and Glauce (Creusa) : revenge of a scorned woman (Euripides, *Medea*) .

5. Ino, Athamas, and Antiphera: death of the illegitimate child of Athamas and Antiphera at the hands of Ino.

6. Dirce, Lycus, and Antiope: Dirce the wife punished Antiope the ex-wife, until Antiope's twin sons by Zeus killed Dirce.

C. Triangle stories: two men and one woman

1. Neoptolemus (Pyrrhus) , Hermione, and Orestes: "love will find a way," as Hermione's rescue by Orestes proves (Ovid, *Heroides* 8) .

2. Agamemnon, Briseis, and Achilles: "what's mine is mine, and what's yours is mine too" (Homer, *Iliad* 1).
3. Aegisthus, Clytemnestra, and Agamemnon: famous last words, "there's no place like home" (Aeschylus, *Agamemnon*).

D. The wicked step-mother

1. Nephele, Athamas, and Ino: Ino intended to kill Phrixus and Helle, Athamas' children by Nephele; saved by the golden-fleeced ram, but death of Helle in sea named for her.
2. Theseus, Hippolytus, and Phaedra: false accusations and unjustified death of Hippolytus (Euripides, *Hippolytus*).
3. Aegeus, Theseus and Medea: near accidental death of Theseus.
4. Phineus, Idaea, and two sons of Phineus: false accusations and unjustified punishment of sons by Phineus.
5. Proetus, Bellerophon, and Anteia: false accusations and unjustified punishment of Bellerophon.
6. Cycnus, Tenes, and Philonome: false accusations and unjustified injury to Tenes by father Cycnus; reconciliation effected.

E. Nightingale, and other bird, stories

1. Zethus, Niobe, and Aedon: jealous Aedon and the death of her own son, Itylus, whose name she calls continually in her transformed nightingale state.
2. Zetes, hamadryad, and Aedon: turned into a nightingale, Aedon continually mourns her son, Aetylus, whom she killed as a suspected go-between for Zetes, her husband and a hamadryad.
3. Polytechnos, Chelidon, and Aedon: Aedon's revenge on Polytechnos, death of their son Itys; all changed into birds.
4. Procne, Tereus, and Philomela: son of Tereus, Itylos (or Itys) killed, cooked and served to father; all changed into birds (Ovid, *Metamorphoses* 6).
5. Caneus, Picus, and Circe: a handsome lad, refusing Circe, changed into a woodpecker; his faithful lover

Caneus, singing her woeful loss, wasted entirely away (Ovid, *Metamorphoses* 14) .

F. Incestuous love

1. Myrrha and her father, Cinyras: unsuspecting father responsible for birth of Adonis (Ovid, *Metamorphoses* 10) .

2. Nyctimene and father, Nyctaeus: unwitting father, upon discovery of truth, foiled in attempt upon Nyctimene's life, as Athena transforms her into an owl.

3. Harpalyce and father, Clymenus: a served-up brother finally halted the advances of the over-zealous father, who had killed Harpalyce's husband; Harpalyce changed into an owl, suicide of Clymenus.

4. Pelopeia and father, Thyestes: birth of Aegisthus, who, despite mother's efforts, lived to avenge Thyestes.

5. Byblis and brother, Caunus: in one version, Byblis committed suicide with the refusal of Caunus; another version states that Byblis, after a long and unsuccessful pursuit of Caunus, was turned into a true fountain of tears (Ovid, *Metamorphoses* 9) .

6. Canace and brother, Macareus: after birth of a child, Canace killed herself at the order of and with the sword of her father, Aeolus; Macareus became a priest of Apollo at Delphi.

7. Oedipus and mother, Jocasta: inadvertent marriage which produced four children and dire consequences.

G. Contests for brides

1. Atalanta and Hippomenes (or Melanion) : the usual fruit of love, the apple, wins the race, life, and love (Ovid, *Metamorphoses* 10) .

2. Hippodamia and Polops: the chariot race in which Myrtilus made the difference.

3. Marpessa and Idas: a contest between Idas and Apollo averted by the choice of Marpessa.

4. Deianira and Heracles: Achelous' loss was Heracles' gain.

5. Pero and Bias: cattle recovered by Bias moo-ved Pero to marriage.

6. Penelope and Odysseus: the contest of the bow proved the "beggar's" return.

H. Miscellaneous tales

1. Narcissus: he had such a good image that he fell in love with it (Ovid, *Metamorphoses* 3).

2. Salmacis: who had her way with Hermaphroditus (Ovid, *Metamorphoses* 4).

3. Melampus: an ancient Tarzan who found the cattle given to Pero, was kept alive for a while by friendly bees, told Iphiclus how to become a father, relieved the madness of the women of Argos, and settled down as a seer in Argos, where he lived for 6 generations.

4. Aepytus: return of the "dead," a mother made happy, and a new king for Messenia.

5. Nisus: his safety-lock (of purple hair) was snipped by his daughter Scylla out of love for King Minos; she was changed into a lark by the gods, and Nisus be-became a hawk (Ovid, *Metamorphoses* 8).

6. Midas: received gift of golden touch from Bacchus and ears of an ass by Apollo (Ovid, *Metamorphoses* 11).

7. Ion: who was nearly killed by Creusa, recognized by her, became king of Athens and ancestor of all Ionians (Euripides, *Ion*).

8. Idomeneus: his fulfilling of a vow to Poseidon made him so hateful to the Cretans that he left Crete for good, (perhaps banished), and spent the rest of his life in Italy.

9. Talos (or Perdix): the nephew of Daedalus who surpassed his uncle in ingenuity and was, for his own safety, changed into a partridge by Athena (Ovid, *Metamorphoses* 8).

10. Tarpeia: who betrayed Rome to the Sabines and received a just, but unexpected, reward of death.

11. Biton and Cleobis: brothers who made their mother the proudest mortal and received from Hera her best reward, a happy death.

12. Dryope: for harming the tree-home of Lotis, she was turned into a tree herself, having just enough time to remind her husband Andaemon to look after their son (Ovid, *Metamorphoses* 9).

The many references to the *Heroides* and the *Metamorphoses* in the numerous stories above emphasize the interest of Ovid in mythical love; his equal interest in Roman, or real, love is apparent in the *Amores,* the *Ars Amatoria,* and the *Remedia Amoris.* It is in the *Metamorphoses,* however, that Ovid displays more than just a casual interest in love or in the psychology of lovers. The many stories do compose a full spectrum of love affairs, but, in addition, they all point to the power of love, that is, the power of Cupid and Venus. Cupid rules all kingdoms, Heaven, Sea, and Lower World, and causes even Venus to fall in love with Adonis (10.525-30). Nowhere is the power of love more detailed than by the long series of stories told by Orpheus himself (10.1-11.84).

Noticeably, the song of Orpheus serves at least two other functions: it introduces Venus as a powerful deity herself while ending the cycle of myth, and it stands as a strong bridge linking the two purely philosophic passages of the *Metamorphoses* (1.5-88 and 15.75-478). As has been shown, all three passages are related, in that they represent the beliefs of the rather amorphous religious philosophy called Orphism. One of the ideas within Orphism held that the oldest god, the god responsible for all creation, was Eros (Love); thus, to Empedocles, Love (Philia) was the force which caused birth and unity, while Strife (Neikos) caused death and dissolution. Ovid, familiar with Orphism, utilizes the Empedoclean scheme of creation in Book 1 and the Orphic-Pythagorean scheme of reincarnation in Book 15. And, in between these passages, stands Book 10, in which Orpheus is the speaker, telling of love and its effects. Love, then, is not only a natural and erotic force; it is, as well, a cosmic and cosmological force the source of creation and re-creation. But Venus is more.

As the latter books of the *Metamorphoses* unfold, we see that the greatest transformation of all is recounted, the rebirth of Troy as Rome. Responsible for this reincarnation is Aeneas, the Trojan son of Anchises and Venus. It is a mother's concern which Venus shows toward Aeneas, his followers, and his de-

scendants. Venus is the mother (Genetrix) of the Romans
generally, and of the Julian line specifically. Lucretius began
his great poem with the words *Aeneadum genetrix* ("mother
of the descendants of Aeneas") referring to Venus, and in
46 B. C. the beautiful temple of Venus Genetrix was dedicated
by Julius Caesar; still later, the largest temple ever built in
Rome was the temple of Venus and Roma. (There is also the
obvious fact that Roma is Amor spelled backward.)

The function of Venus in the *Metamorphoses,* therefore, is
threefold, as the protector and mother of the Romans, as the
cosmological force in the universe, and as the powerful erotic
force. In the latter role, she is a power not to be scorned or
ignored, as so many stories illustrate. Those who do ignore or
scorn her frequently suffer the fate of being turned to stone,
thereby becoming completely insensible. Of all the images used
in the *Metamorphoses,* the most common is that of stone, and,
in most of its occurrences, the image of stone is linked with the
theme of love. There are numerous tales to warn any who think
ill of love to beware of petrifaction; yet, there is one story to
show the reverse, *viz.,* that proper attention to love can result
in stone's being given life. That is the story of Pygmalion, in
Book 10.

The Pygmalion episode is, in fact, the converging point for
Ovid's image of stone, his theme of the power of love, and his
belief in the power of art, i.e., the fine arts. The episode, almost
entirely Ovid's own creation, is set in a series showing love
affairs with unhappy endings, from Orpheus and Eurydice to
Venus and Adonis. And, in the immediately preceding episode,
the Propoetides, because of their scorning of Venus, were made
prostitutes by her and then turned into stone. But here is
Pygmalion, a sculptor and a scorner of women; he creates a
statue of a woman so beautiful that he falls in love with it, and
because of his change of heart, the statue changes to a real
woman who eventually bears Paphos, the child of perfect love.
This was a miracle, the sort of miracle which only the skill of
the artist and the power of love could effect.

Finally, the very position of the Pygmalion story indicates its
importance to Ovid: the ratio between the 7377 preceding
verses and the 4554 succeeding verses (exclusive of the 9-line
epilogue) is 0.618, the Golden Section ratio, found in Virgil,
Horace, Lucan, and other Latin authors. The same principle

has been discovered in other civilizations and in other media, for it seems to be the most pleasing artistic principle; the greater part is to the lesser as the sum of the two is to the greater,

$$\frac{m}{M} = \frac{M}{M + m}.$$

The epilogue of the *Metamorphoses* is the final signature of Ovid upon the work. As a creative artist, he predicts optimistically that his work will live on, though his own life ends. (Certainly, Ovid would have subscribed to the motto, Ars Longa, Vita Brevis.) Thus far his prediction has proved true; hopefully, it will continue to be true.

(For further information on the above points, read L. P. Wilkinson, *Ovid Surveyed;* George Duckworth, *Structural Patterns and Proportions in Virgil's Aeneid;* W. C. Stephens, "Cupid and Venus in Ovid's *Metamorphoses*," *Transactions of the American Philological Association*, Vol. 89 (1958) ; and D. F. Bauer, "The Function of Pygmalion in the *Metamorphoses*," *Transactions of the American Philological Association*, Vol. 93 (1962) .)

CHAPTER 10
A Brief History of Greek Art
and Its Use of Mythology

Since mythology provided Greek artists and sculptors with such a varied store-house of subject-matter, it will be beneficial to trace briefly the development of Greek art and to indicate, though in a limited degree, its reliance upon mythology. Obviously, we cannot here present a thorough exposition, complete with a listing of all works of art whose subjects were drawn from the myths. We can, however, state a few generalizations (perhaps not too sweeping or wrath-provoking), and mention some of the great artists and their treatment of mythological subjects. It would be idle to speculate on what Greek art would have been like without mythology, although a slight suggestion might be found in the very early vases, which were covered with all sorts of linear and floral designs and figures of animals. The artists did have mythology, and mythology did create challenges for men of talent and skill; the result was a happy fusion which continues to prove Keats' paraphrase of Euripides, "A thing of beauty is a joy forever," (*Bacchae* 881). (For a fuller treatment of myths in sculpture, see Walter Agard's *Classical Myths in Sculpture;* other books, of a more general nature and presenting a survey of Greek art, include *Masterpieces of Greek Art* by R. V. Schoder, S. J.; *A Handbook of Greek Art* by G. M. A. Richter; and, *Greek Art* by John Boardman. Jean Seznec's *The Survival of the Pagan Gods* shows the use of mythology in the art of the Renaissance, and *Mythology in Prints,* edited by L. M. Prindle, is a collection of illustrations, for the *Metamorphoses,* dating from 1497 to 1824. Books of all sizes, levels, and prices are available, ranging upward from two Pocket Books, *The Pocket Book of Greek Art* by Thomas Craven, and *Gods and Goddesses in Art and Legend* by H. J. Wechsler.)

I. Minoan-Mycenaean Period (c. 2000-c. 1100): early Aegean cultural homogeneity which, about 1600, broke in two.

  A. On Crete: elaborate palaces, bright wall paintings, fine jewelry, delicate vases; figures of plants and animals used for decoration; Linear A (throughout Crete).

  B. At Mycenae: citadel surrounded by strong walls, Lion Gate, beehive tombs; art works derived from the Cretan or strongly influenced by it; Linear B (on mainland and at Cnossus).

II. Proto-Geometric and Geometric Periods (c. 1100-c. 700): after Dorian invasion; pottery about the only art form; little aesthetic interest, but many decorations, especially dots, wavy lines, zig-zags, triangles, animals, birds, and triangular-chested men. Homer wrote of the earlier Mycenaean age, in his style utilizing geometric patterns (see Cedric Whitman, *Homer and the Heroic Tradition*); Hesiod wrote of the hard times in which he lived, and an Eastern contemporary, Amos, voiced the same plaints.

III. Orientalizing Period (c. 700-c. 600): contacts with East renewed and apparent in all art forms; small statues of bronze, ivory and clay show new techniques; marble statuary appears, peripteral temples utilizing Doric style begin to evolve, and gold jewelry reappears; Corinth and Athens become centers of pottery industry, with decorations of flowers, lotus and pal-mettes, griffins, sphinxes, and lions; human figures more life-like though still profile or frontal.

IV. Archaic Period (c. 600-c. 480): an age of discovery, political, social, and economic progress; invention of coinage aids development of commerce and industry.

  A. Architecture: Ionic style evolves, as Doric becomes more perfected: temples of Apollo at Corinth, Hera at Samos, Artemis at Ephesus.

  B. Sculpture: free-standing works, life-size or over, with Egyptian influences: smile, almond-shaped eyes, "mat"-hair, figure erect, facing forward, left leg slightly advanced hands held stiffly at side.

   1. kouros: nude, male.
   2. kore: draped, female.
   3. seated draped figure, male or female.

    4. relief sculpture: motion indicated by half-kneeling or half-reclining stance; tomb-stones.

C. Pottery: centers at Corinth, Sparta, Athens, colonies in Italy and Sicily.

    1. black-figure ware of Athens: human figures in action dominate decoration, flowers or geometric patterns used at base and neck: figures rather stiff and in profile. Recognized masters of the style include Exekias, Nicosthenes, Psiax, Rycroft Painter, Andocides Painter, Amasis Painter, Nessos Painter; the Francois Vase (c. 570).

    2. red-figure ware of Athens (developed c. 530) : more freedom for figures and detail, more individuality by artists. Masters include Berlin Painter, Douris, Pan Painter, Chicago Painter, Pasiades, Sotades, Euthymides; some artists, such as the Andocides Painter, excel in both black-figure and red-figure techniques.

D. Others: gem engraving, coins, figurines; the Vix crater.

V. Classical Period (c. 480-c. 400): the Golden (or Periclean) Age, between the Persian and Peloponnesian Wars; literature and art flourish, as Athens becomes leader of sea-empire and Sparta builds land-empire; humanism, rationalism, idealism.

A. Architecture: earlier "trial-and-error" techniques end in triumph: Parthenon, Hephaesteum, Zeus at Olympia, Erechtheum, Propylaea, Athena Nike, Apollo at Bassae (earliest example of Corinthian column).

B. Sculpture: from early works, such as the Discus Thrower of Myron, through the greatest name of the field, Phidias, to the creator of ideal proportions, Polyclitus; temple sculptures, relief sarcophagi, "Ludovisi Throne."

C. Pottery: red-figure ware still dominates, though others, such as white-ground *lekythoi,* become popular: individual artists and schools flourish.

D. Others: beginning of mosaic technique; gem-engraving, in which Dexamenus excels.

VI. Fourth Century (c. 400-c. 323): the age of the individual, as philosophy, science, and oratory question old ideas and beliefs; culture thrives at Pergamum, and Alexandria is founded, as the world shrinks with Alexander's conquests.

A. Architecture: temple of Asclepius at Epidaurus, Apollo at Delphi, Artemis at Ephesus (new); Mausoleum at Halicarnassus.

B. Sculpture: Cephisodotus, Scopas, Praxiteles, and Lysippus are the recognized masters; private commissions become more common, and sculptors respond; portrait sculpture.

C. Pottery and Others: new centers of pottery-making compete successfully with old centers; Apelles, the most famous painter in antiquity, serves as Alexander's private portraitist; coins of silver, bronze, and gold show refinements; personal jewelry exhibits elegance and taste.

VII. Hellenistic Period (c. 323-c. 100 B. C.): Greek culture affects the rest of the world, as that of the rest of the world affects Greece; trademarks of the age are individualism, realism, and erudition; advance of Rome heralds political decline and dependence of Greece, Macedonia, and other Eastern areas.

A. Architecture: Stoa of Attalus at Athens; Altar of Zeus at Pergamum.

B. Sculpture: Nike of Samothrace, Dying Gaul, Boxer, Aphrodite of Melos, Laocoön.

C. Pottery and Others: red-figure ware wears out; mosaics popular; glass vases and cameo techniques developed: Farnese Plate, Portland Vase; terracotta figurines, especially those from Tanagra, in great demand for home or personal enjoyment.

Herodotus observed that Homer and Hesiod had given the Greeks their gods; this gift, with formal recognition by Pisistratus, was taken seriously by the Athenians, who built temporary homes for their gods and statues in praise to their gods. Thus, architecture and sculpture benefited as much from Homer and Hesiod as did literature. Vase painters too drew heavily from Homer and Hesiod, depicting not only gods, but heroes of the earlier Bronze Age. The exploits of the great hero, Heracles, and of various local heroes, such as Theseus in Athens, also provided rich material for artists. Finally, there was the challenge presented to artists by the horrible actions of various monsters, such as centaurs and Gorgons. Mythology, in short, that common body of knowledge, was the *sine qua non,* if not the *summum bonum,* of much artistic endeavor—from the Parthenon to the earliest attempt at a temple for a deity, from

the most monumental statue to the most delicate figurine,
from the best paintings of the pottery decorators to the colorful
floor mosaicist, from the drinking cups and battle armor to the
filigree jewelry and perfume bottles.

The following list, it is hoped, will suffice to illustrate the
artists' reliance on mythology, providing for them examples
to be initiated in:

A. Architecture
1. Temples of Zeus at Olympia, designed by Libo (6th
    and 5th centuries), at Cyrene (c. 540), at Acragas
    (Agrigentum) (c. 500-c. 460), at Athens (174 B. C.-
    131 A. D.) ; Altar of Zeus and Athena at Pergamum
    (c. 200-c. 150) ; Stoa of Zeus at Athens (1st and 2nd
    centuries A. D.)
2. Temples of Hera at Olympia (c. 600), at Paestum
    (c. 530), the river Sele (c. 520-500), at Paestum
    (c. 460).
3. Temples of Apollo at Corinth (c. 540), at Delphi
    (c. 520) at Bassae (c. 425), at Delphi (c. 360-330),
    at Didyma (c. 315).
4. Temples of Athena at Athens (c. 530), at Paestum
    (c. 510), at Athens (Parthenon, 447-438), at Athens
    (Nike, 427-424), at Tegea (c. 390), at Priene (c.340-
    334) ; Altar of Zeus and Athena at Pergamum
    (c.200-c. 150).
5. Temples to Artemis, at Corcyra (c. 600), at Ephe-
    sus (c. 550, rebuilt c. 350), at Sardis (c. 350-300), at
    Magnesia (rebuilt c. 150).
6. Temple of Hephaestus at Athens (c. 449).
7. Temples of Poseidon at Sunium (c. 440), at Athens
    (with Erechtheus and Athena, the Erechtheum,
    421-406).
8. Temple of Asclepius at Epidaurus (c. 380).
9. Temple of Hecate at Lagina (c. 150).
10. Theaters of Dionysos at Athens (5th century), at
    Epidaurus (c. 350).
11. Temple of Ares at Athens (5th century).

B. Sculpture
1. Gorgon, Temple of Artemis at Corcyra (c. 600).
2. Hera of Samos (c. 575-550).
3. 3-headed Typhon, Athenian pediment (c. 560-550).

4. Europa and the Bull, metope at Selinus (c. 560).
5. Heracles and the Cercopes, metope at Selinus (c. 540).
6. Various Labors of Heracles and events from Trojan War, metope at Sele (c. 575-550).
7. Apollo and Heracles, pediment at Delphi (c. 530-525).
8. Zeus and Athena vs. Giants, pediment at Athens (c. 525-520).
9. Gods vs. Giants, frieze at Siphnian Treasury (c. 530-525).
10. Exploits of Heracles and Theseus, metope at Delphi (c. 520).
11. Harpies (or Sirens) carrying off souls of the dead, from tomb-stone at Xanthos (early 5th century).
12. Athena, Greeks vs. Trojans, Heracles, pediments at Aegina (c. 500-480).
13. Zeus carrying away Ganymede, terra-cotta from Olympia (c. 500-475).
14. Apollo, Zeus, Labors of Heracles, pediments and metopes, at Olympia (465-457); seated Zeus, cult statue at Olympia by Phidias.
15. Omphalos Apollo at Athens (c. 450).
16. Poseidon at Artemisium (c. 470-450).
17. Birth of Aphrodite, relief now at Rome (c. 470-460).
18. Mourning Athena, relief at Athens (c. 470-460).
19. Artemis and Actaeon, metope at Selinus (c. 470-460).
20. Marsyas by Myron (c. 460-450).
21. Contest of Athena and Poseidon, Birth of Athena: Helios, 3 Fates, Theseus, pediments at Athens (Parthenon, c. 438-431).
22. Lapiths vs. Centaurs, Greeks vs. Amazons, Fall of Troy, metopes at Athens (Parthenon, c. 447-443).
23. Athena Parthenos by Phidias (c. 447-439).
24. Athena Lemnia by Phidias (c. 440).
25. Hera by Polyclitus (c. 440).
26. Amazon at Ephesus by Polyclitus (c. 440); by Phidias (c. 440-430).
27. "Venus Genetrix" by unknown sculptor (c. 430-400).
28. Demeter, Triptolemus and persephone, votive relief at Eleusis (c. 440).
29. Hermes, Orpheus and Eurydice; Heracles, Theseus

and Pirithous; Medea; Heracles and 2 Hesperides, votive reliefs (?) (c. 425).

30. Asclepius, relief at Epidaurus (c. 400-380).
31. Eirene and Plutos by Cephisodotus (c. 375-370).
32. Aphrodite of Cnidus; Apollo the Lizard-Slayer; Eros; Satyr; Artemis; Hermes with Infant Dionysos; Apollo; Marsyas and Muses—all by Praxiteles (c. 350-330).
33. Heracles; Zeus; Helios by Lysippus.
34. Demeter of Cnidus by unknown sculptor (c. 350).
35. Apollo at Belvedere by unknown sculptor (c. 350).
36. Themis at Athens (c. 300-250).
37. Niobids by unknown sculptor (c. 300).
38. Ariadne by unknown sculptor (c. 240).
39. Poseidon of Melos; Aphrodite of Melos by unknown sculptors (c. 200).
40. Laocoön by Agesander, Polydorus and Athenadorus (c. 160-130); discovered in Rome in 1506, it made a great impact upon Renaissance sculptors, including Michelangelo.

C. Vase-Paintings: these do not need individual listings, since the above sculptures indicate clearly the variety of subjects. One excellent work should perhaps be mentioned, the cylix interior done by Exekias c. 540; here he translated the Homeric Hymn to Dionysos into a beautiful and balanced scene in which Dionysos transforms the pirates into dolphins and the ship's mast into grape-clusters. Generally speaking, favorite topics for vase-painters were individual combats of heroes, adventures of Odysseus, sea-myths and various exploits of Heracles and Theseus. Lest there be any doubt in the mind of the viewer, the painter frequently identified his characters by name, thereby setting forth the scene or action.

With regard to Roman utilization of myths in art, it might be said that, in sculpture, at least, their best contribution was imitation of Greek originals; it can be truthfully said in many cases, "By the Roman copies, ye shall know them." As noted earlier, however, temples were built in Rome and throughout the empire to gods and goddesses. References are frequent in Latin literature to these temples, for example: Jupiter Optimus Maximus, Jupiter Stator, Juno Moneta, Janus, Vesta, Saturn (where the state treasury rested), Diana, Venus Genetrix,

Apollo, Mars Ultor, Castor and Pollux, Pantheon, Venus and Roma. There does seem to be an inescapable feeling that the hearts of the Romans weren't entirely in this sort of enterprise; perhaps their feelings were echoed by the legalistic attitude with which they sacrificed to the gods, as summarized by the formula, *do ut des,* "I give that you may give." To the practical Romans, contracts were necessary even with the gods.

CHAPTER 11

Myths in Other Areas

I. The Heavens
A. Stars and Constellations of Spring and Summer
   1. Ursa Major, the Big Bear: Callisto, a lover of Zeus whom Artemis or Zeus himself had changed into a bear. Zeus rescued Callisto as she was about to be killed by Arcas, her son by Zeus; Hera, resentful of Callisto's having been put in the heavens, persuaded Poseidon never to allow Callisto to set in his waters.
   2. Leo the Lion: probably the Nemean Lion, killed by Heracles as his first Labor.
   3. Hydra the Water-Snake; Corvus the Crow; Crater the Cup; Noctua the Owl: the dragon of Aetes, killed by Jason; the bird sacred to Apollo, and whose shape he assumed during the war with the Giants; the cup of Apollo or Dionysos; the Roman word for owl, from the same root as the name of Nyctimene who, after incest with her father, was changed into an owl by Athena.
   4. Scorpio the Scorpion: the scorpion which, Ovid said, killed Orion after he had boasted that he could overcome any animal on earth.
   5. Boötes, the Herdsman: the protector of the Big Bear, either Lycaon, the father of Callisto, or Arcas, son of Callisto.
   6. Corona Borealis (Northern Crown) : the 7-star crown given to Ariadne by Dionysos.
   7. Hercules: Heracles the greatest Pan-Hellenic hero-god.
   8. Opiuchus, the Serpent-Bearer; Serpeus, the Serpent: often identified as Asclepius with a snake, the latter

considered by the ancients to possess great wisdom and power of healing.

9. Sagittarius, the Archer: the centaur Chiron, who instructed so many of the Greek heroes (e.g., Heracles and Jason).

10. Lyra, the Lyre: the instrument invented by Hermes, who gave it to Apollo, who in turn gave it to Orpheus.

11. Aquila, the Eagle: the bird of Zeus (Jupiter, Jove); Ovid referred to it as Merops, a king of the island Cos, who had been changed into an eagle.

12. Cygnus, the Swan: variously identified as the son of Ares who was killed by Heracles, the son of Poseidon killed by Achilles, the brother of Phaëthon, the bird of Venus, or Orpheus put near his favorite lyre.

B. Stars and Constellations of Fall and Winter

1. Gemini, the Twins: Castor and Pollux, the Spartan heroes, brothers of Helen and Clytemnestra.

2. Canis Major, and Great Dog: variously identified as Laelaps, the hound of Actaeon, the hound of Procris, the swift dog given by Cephalus to Aurora, or the dog of Orion.

3. Auriga, the Charioteer: Erichthonius, the half-man, half-serpent son of Hephaestus, but reared by Athena; as king of Athens, he instituted worship of Athena, and, because of his difficulty of locomotion, invented the 4-horse chariot.

4. Orion, the Hunter: the giant who was associated closely with Artemis and the central figure in many myths.

5. Taurus, the Bull: the bull, really Zeus, who carried Europa away to Crete.

6. Perseus, the Champion: the hero, son of Zeus and Danaë.

7. Cassiopeia, the Queen: wife of King Cepheus of Ethiopia and mother of Andromeda; her boasts led to Andromeda's being offered to the sea-monster of Poseidon, but Perseus rescued and married her; Poseidon put Cassiopeia in the heavens in such a position that, at times, she is hanging upside down.

8. Andromeda, the Chained Lady: chained to a rock to appease Poseidon but rescued and married by Perseus.

9. Pegasus, the Flying Horse: sprung from Medusa's blood, ridden by Bellerophon.

10. Aquarius, the Water-Bearer: sometimes identified as Ganymede, the Trojan prince seized by (the eagle of) Zeus to become his cup-bearer.

11. Cetus, the Whale: the monster sent by Poseidon to ravage Ethiopia, killed by Perseus who then married Andromeda, the intended victim of Cetus.

12. Ursa Minor, the Little Bear; Draco, the Dragon: the nymph who nursed Zeus on Mt. Ida in Crete; the snake taken from the Giants by Athena, or the monster sacred to Ares and killed by Jason.

C. Planets ("Wanderers"): Mercury, Venus, Earth, Mars, Jupiter, Saturn, Uranus, Neptune, Pluto. Noticeably, each planet was given an appropriate name or description:

1. Mercury, the closest to the Sun, has a year of 88 days and thus is the fastest.

2. Venus, the brightest planet in the heavens and surrounded by a lovely (gaseous) color.

3. Earth, though lacking a mythological name, is still the most fundamental planet to us.

4. Mars, the "red planet," associated with blood and war, one of its "seas" named after the Amazons.

5. Jupiter, the largest planet with its own circling moons, one of which is named Ganymede.

6. Saturn, the second largest planet, sixth in distance from the Sun (with Jupiter fifth), known for its 3 concentric rings composed of thousands of stars.

7. Uranus, seventh in distance from the Sun (father of Saturn and grandfather of Jupiter).

8. Neptune, third largest planet, eighth from the Sun, with a trident as its symbol.

9. Pluto, ninth from the Sun, the outermost planet and, therefore, farthest from light.

D. Zodiac ("Circle of Animals"): (those listed above in A or B will not be dealt with in detail here)

1. Aquarius, the Water-Bearer: B10 above.

2. Pisces, the Fish: the forms taken by Aphrodite and

Eros, as they fled the attack of Typhon against the gods.

3. Aries, the Ram: the ram with the Golden Fleece which rescued Phrixus and Helle (though Helle fell off and drowned in the sea, which was then named for her, Hellespont).

4. Taurus, the Bull: B5 above.

5. Gemini, the Twins: B1 above.

6. Cancer, the Crab: the crab sent by Hera against Heracles when the latter was fighting Hydra; Heracles crushed it with his feet, and Hera put it in the heavens.

7. Leo, the Lion: the Nemean Lion, killed by Heracles.

8. Virgo, the Virgin: Kore, or Persephone, (Ceres) who was carried to the Underworld by Hades and split her time between husband and Mother (Demeter).

9. Libra, the Scales (or Balance): perhaps originally the claws of the Scorpion (Scorpio); came to represent equality of day and night.

10. Scorpio, the Scorpion: A4 above.

11. Sagittarius, the Archer: A9 above.

12. Capricorn, the Goat: Amalthea, the goat-nymph who nursed Zeus in Crete (cf. B12 above).

E. Other Constellations

1. Ara, the Altar: variously identified as the altar raised by Zeus at the time the gods fought with the Titans, the *thymele* of Dionysos, or the hearth of Hestia.

2. Argo, the Ship: the ship which carried Jason and his followers in quest of the Golden Fleece. Parts of this constellation include Carina, the Keel, Puppis, the Stern, and Canopus, the brightest star in the Southern skies.

3. Canis Minor, the Lesser Dog (cf. B2 above): variously identified as a hound of Actaeon, of Artemis, or Orion.

4. Centaurus, the Centaur: specifically identified as Pholus who was kind to Heracles, or Chiron who taught Heracles and other heroes.

5. Cepheus, the King: king of Ethiopia, husband of Cassiopeia, father of Andromeda, petrified by head of Medusa, carried by Perseus.

6. Corvus, the Crow: the bird sacred to Apollo and the shape he assumed at the time of the gods' battle with the Giants.

7. Delphinus, the Dolphin: any dolphin, since dolphins were so popular for their philanthropy; specifically, Ovid identified it as the dolphin which persuaded Amphitrite to become Poseidon's wife.

8. Equuleus, the Foal: close to, and associated with, Pegasus (B9 above).

9. Eridanus, the River: identified as Homer's River of Ocean, the Rhone, or the Po; the grieving sisters of Phaëthon were turned into poplars along its banks, since it had received Phaëthon's smoking body.

10. Hyades: 5, 6, or 7 daughters of Atlas and Aethra who grieved so much over their brother, Hyas, who had been killed by a boar, that Zeus put them in the heavens near Taurus.

11. Lepus, the Hare: situated near Orion, the Hunter and his Hound, Canis Major.

12. Phoenix, the Bird: the legendary bird of Egypt, one of a kind, which after 500 or 600 years, cremated itself; out of its ashes a new phoenix arose.

13. Pleiades: 7 daughters of Atlas and Pleione, sometimes called the Seven Sisters; put into the heavens to escape Orion or because they grieved so at the loss of their half-sisters, the Hyades (10 above).

14. Pyxis, the Compass: associated with the Argo, ship and constellation, as is Vela, the Veil (or Sails).

15. Sagitta, the Arrow: variously identified as the arrow of Heracles, Apollo, or Eros.

16. Others have names derived from Latin words but unconnected with any particular mythological person, animal, or object: e.g., Pictor, the Painter; Lupus, the Wolf; Musca, the Fly; Volans, the Flying.

(For further, and often fascinating, information, read *Star Names: Their Lore and Meaning* by R. H. Allen; though old, it still is valuable for anyone interested in this subject.)

II. Literature: it would be nearly a life-long task to indicate the extent to which Western literature has made use of mythology as subject-matter, symbols, or allusions. Certainly, no one can pursue a serious study of the literature of any Western country without familiarizing himself with classical mythology (and the *Bible*). Some works which the student of English literature might refer to are these: *Bibliography of Greek Myth in English Poetry* by Helen H. Law; *The Classical Tradition* by Gilbert Highet; *Mythology and the Renaissance Tradition in English Poetry* and *Mythology and the Romantic Tradition in English Poetry* by Douglas Bush; and, the most comprehensive work to date, *Classical Myths in English Literature* by Dan S. Norton and Peters Rushton. At a more elementary level, and of recent date, there is *Myths and Their Meaning* by Max J. Herzberg.

III. Vocabulary: listed below are some words derived from names of deities; further searching in a good, standard dictionary will add to the list and increase one's allusive vocabulary:

artemisia	floral	iridescent	peony
athenaeum	geology	Junoesque	phosphorus
auroral	gigantic	jovial	plutocracy
boreal	hebephrenia	lunatic	Plutonic
cereal	heliotrope	martial	protean
dianthus	herculean	mercurial	saturnine
dionaea	hermetic	museum	selenography
eosin	hygienic	neptunium	titanic
euthanasia	hymeneal	oceanography	uranium
faun	hypnotic	palladium	vestal
favonian	irenics	panic	zephyr

Select Bibliography

Of the works listed below, many are available in paper-bound editions, some are rather scholarly, others are for younger readers, and a few are old familiar stand-bys.

Addison, Julia. Classic Myths in Art

Agard, Walter. Classical Myths in Sculpture

Asimov, Isaac. Words from Myths

Bowra, M. C. The Greek Experience

Bray, Frank C. The World of Myths

Bulfinch, Thomas. The Age of Fable

Bush, Douglas. Mythology and the Renaissance Tradition

————. Mythology and the Romantic Tradition in English Poetry

Campbell, Joseph. Pagan and Christian Mysteries

————. Hero with a Thousand Faces

————. Masks of God (2 vols.)

Cassirer, Ernst. Language and Myth

Chase, Richard. Quest for Myth

Colum, Padraic. Golden Fleece, and Heroes who Lived Before Achilles

————. Myths of the World

Cook, A. B. Zeus, A Study in Ancient Religions

Cottrell, Leonard. The Bull of Minos

Cox, George. Tales of Ancient Greece

Cumont, Franz. After Life in Roman Paganism

Dickinson, G. Lowes. The Greek View of Life

Eliade, Mircea. Cosmos and History

Fairbanks, Arthur. The Mythology of Greece and Rome

Finley, M. I. The Ancient Greeks

Frazer, Sir J. G. The Golden Bough (Abridged)

Gayley, Charles M. Classic Myths in English Literature and Art

Grant, Michael. Myths of the Greeks and Romans

Graves, Robert. Greek Gods and Heroes

————. The Greek Myths (2 vols.)

Green, Roger L. Tales of the Greek Heroes

_____. The Tale of Troy
Grimal, Pierre. Dictionnaire de la Mythologie Grecque et Romaine
Guthrie, W. K. C. The Greeks and Their Gods
_____. Religion and Mythology of the Greeks
Halliday, W. R. Indo-European Folk-Tales and Greek Legend
Hamilton, Edith. Mythology
Harrison, Jane. Mythology
_____. Prolegomena to the Study of Greek Religion
Herzberg, Max J. Myths and Their Meanings
Jung, Carl G. and Kerényi, C. Essays on a Science of Mythology
Kerényi, C. The Gods of the Greeks
Kirkwood, Gordon M. Short Guide to Classical Mythology
Kitto, H. D. F. Form and Meaning in Drama
_____. Greek Tragedy
_____. The Greeks
Kramer, Samuel N. Mythologies of the Ancient World
_____. Sumerian Mythology
Lang, Andrew. Myth, Ritual and Religion (2 vols.)
Law, Helen. Bibliography of Greek Myth in English Poetry
Malinowski, Bronislaw. Myth in Primitive Psychology
_____. Magic, Science and Religion and Other Essays
Moncrieff, A. R. H. Classical Myth and Legend
Muller, H. J. The Loom of History
_____. The Uses of the Past
New Century Classical Handbook
Nilsson, Martin P. Greek Folk Religion
_____. The Mycenaean Origin of Greek Mythology
Norton, Dan C. and Rushton, Peters. Classical Myths in English Literature
Osgood, Charles G. The Classical Mythology of Milton's English Poems
Otto, Walter F. The Homeric Gods
Oxford Classical Dictionary
Oxford Companion to Classical Literature
Parkes, H. B. Gods and Men
Prindle, L. M. Mythology in Prints
Raglan, Lord. The Hero: A Study in Tradition, Myth, and Drama
Rank, Otto. Myth of the Birth of the Hero and Other Essays
Rose, H. J. A Handbook of Greek Mythology

_____. Gods and Heroes of the Greeks
_____. Religion in Greece and Rome
Rouse, W. H. D. Gods, Heroes and Men of Ancient Greece
Schwab, Gustav. Gods and Heroes
Seltman, Charles. The Twelve Olympians
Seznec, Jean. The Survival of the Pagan Gods
Warner, Rex. Men and Gods
_____. Greeks and Trojans
_____. The Vengeance of the Gods
Wechsler, H. J. Gods and Goddesses in Art and Legend